china

To Reuben, who married me before I learned to cook.

Completely revised and updated in 2011
First published in 1976

This edition published in 2013 by Hardie Grant Books

Hardie Grant Books (Australia)
Ground Floor, Building 1
658 Church Street
Richmond, Victoria 3121
www.hardiegrant.com.au

Hardie Grant Books (UK)
Dudley House, North Suite
34–35 Southampton Street
London WC2E 7HF
www.hardiegrant.co.uk

A Cataloguing-in-Publication entry is available from the catalogue of the National Library of
Australia at www.nla.gov.au
The Complete Asian Cookbook: China
ISBN 978 1 74270 682 5

Publishing Director: Paul McNally
Project Editor: Rihana Ries
Editor: Ariana Klepac
Design Manager: Heather Menzies
Design Concept: Murray Batten
Typesetting: Megan Ellis
Photographer: Alan Benson
Stylist: Vanessa Austin
Production: Todd Rechner

Colour reproduction by Splitting Image Colour Studio
Printed and bound in China by 1010 Printing International Limited

Find this book on **Cooked.**

THE
Complete
Asian
COOKBOOK

china

CHARMAINE SOLOMON

hardie grant books
MELBOURNE · LONDON

Contents

Foreword

Just as France has its robust country fare as well as its subtle haute cuisine, so too does Asia have a range of culinary delights that can be simple, complex, fiery, mild, tantalising — and compulsive! Not all Asian food is exotic or wildly unusual. Noodle and rice dishes are as commonplace as the pastas and potatoes of the West. Many of the ingredients will be familiar to anyone who knows their way around a kitchen. The main differences have arisen just as they have arisen in other parts of the world — through the use of available ingredients. Thus there is a reliance on some herbs and spices less well known in the West. Meat is often replaced by the nutritious by-products of the soy bean and by protein-rich fish sauces and shrimp pastes.

True, some of the more unusual ingredients take a little getting used to. But once you have overcome what resistance you may have towards the idea of raw fish or dried shrimp paste or seaweed, you'll find that these (and other) ingredients are no less delicious than — and certainly as exciting as — those you use in your favourite dishes.

The introduction to this book will give you a good idea of what to expect in the way of out-of-the-ordinary ingredients. Almost without exception, those called for are readily available in most large supermarkets or Asian grocery stores; in the rare case they are not, suitable substitutes have been given.

Those of you already familiar with Chinese cuisine will, I hope, find recipes to interest and excite you in these pages; and I think you will be tempted to explore dishes and ingredients with which you are less well acquainted. For those of you who are coming to Chinese cooking for the first time, I have taken care to make sure the essential steps are clear and precise, with detailed instructions on the following pages for cooking the much-used ingredients (such as rice, noodles and chilli), and pointers on how to joint a chicken, portion fish and select and season a wok.

For most recipes the names have been given in romanised Chinese, followed by the English name in smaller type. In the case of this book, the language used is Cantonese, for the cooking of Kwangtung Province is the Chinese cuisine best known in the West.

Eating for health

Most Asian food is healthy. Many spices and ingredients such as garlic and ginger have proven health-giving properties. However, with today's emphasis on weight control I have made modifications in the quantity and type of fat used for cooking. I have found it is possible to get very good results using almost half the amount of fat called for in many traditional dishes.

All of these recipes are adaptable to low-fat diets with very little sacrifice of flavour, since most of the exotic tastes come from herbs, spices and sauces.

Cooking with a wok

If I had to choose one cooking pan to be marooned on a desert island with, I'd choose a wok. It would cope with any kind of food that happened to be available. In it you can boil, braise, fry and steam, and while you can do all these things in pans you already possess, the wok is almost indispensable for the stir-frying technique that many Asian dishes call for. Because of its rounded shape and high, flaring sides you can toss with abandon and stir-fry ingredients without their leaping over the sides; and because the wok is made of thin iron you get the quick, high heat necessary to much Asian cooking.

Though a wok is best used with gas, it is possible to get good results with electricity. Because quick, high heat is required in stir-frying, turn the hotplate on to the highest heat and place the wok directly on it; it is possible to buy woks with a flat base for better contact, or invest in an electric wok where the heating element is built into the pan. The 30–35 cm (12–14 in) wok is most useful. You can cook small quantities in a large wok, but not vice versa.

The wok made of stainless steel is a modern innovation, but a modestly priced iron wok heats up quickly and evenly and, if you remember to dry it well after washing, it will not rust.

Before use, an iron wok must be seasoned. Prepare it by washing thoroughly in hot water and detergent. Some woks, when new, have a lacquer-like coating, which must be removed by almost filling the wok with water, adding about 2 tablespoons bicarbonate of soda (baking soda) and boiling for about 15 minutes. This softens the coating and it can be scrubbed off with a fine scourer. If some of the coating still remains, repeat the process until the wok is free from any lacquer on the inside. To season the new wok, dry it well, put over gentle heat and, when the metal heats up, wipe over the entire inner surface with some crumpled paper towel dipped in peanut oil. Repeat a number of times with more oil-soaked paper until the paper stays clean. Allow to cool. Your wok is now ready for use.

After cooking in it, do not scrub the wok with steel wool or abrasives of any kind. Soak in hot water to soften any remaining food, then rub gently with a sponge, using hot water and detergent – this preserves the surface. Make sure the wok is quite dry, because if moisture stays left in the pan it will rust. Heat the wok gently to ensure complete dryness, then rub over the inside surface with lightly oiled paper. A well-used wok will soon turn black, but this is normal – and the more a wok is used, the better it is to cook in.

Deep-frying

A wok is an efficient pan for deep-frying as it has a wider surface area than a regular frying pan. Be sure that the wok is sitting securely on the stove. Fill the wok no more than two-thirds full and heat the oil over medium heat.

To check the temperature for deep-frying, use a kitchen thermometer if you have one – on average, 180°C (350°F) is the correct temperature. To test without a thermometer, a cube of bread dropped into the oil will brown in 15 seconds at 180°C (350°F), and in 10 seconds if the temperature is 190°C (375°F).

The higher temperature may be suitable to use for foods that don't have great thickness, but if something needs to cook through, such as chicken pieces, use a lower temperature of around 160°C (320°F) – in this case a cube of bread will take nearly 30 seconds to brown. If the temperature is not hot enough, the food will absorb oil and become greasy. If you overheat the oil it could catch fire.

Use refined peanut oil, light olive oil, canola or rice bran oil and lower the food in gently with tongs or a slotted spoon so as not to splash yourself with hot oil. Removing the fried food to a colander lined with crumpled paper towel will help to remove any excess oil.

After cooling, oil may be poured through a fine metal skimmer and stored in an airtight jar away from the light. It may be used within a month or so, adding fresh oil to it when heating. After a couple of uses, it will need to be disposed of properly.

Chillies

Fresh chillies are used in most Asian food. If mild flavouring is required, simply wash the chilli and add it to the dish when simmering, then lift out and discard the chilli before serving. But if you want the authentic fiery quality of the dish, you need to seed and chop the chillies first. To do this, remove the stalk of each chilli and cut in half lengthways to remove the central membrane and seeds – the seeds are the hottest part of the chilli.

If you handle chillies without wearing gloves, wash your hands thoroughly with soap and warm water afterwards. Chillies can be so hot that even two or three good washings do not stop the tingling sensation, which can go on for hours. If this happens, remember to keep your hands well away from your eyes, lips or where the skin is especially sensitive. If you have more chillies than you need, they can be wrapped in plastic wrap and frozen, then added to dishes and used without thawing.

Dried chillies come in many shapes and sizes. Generally I use the large variety. If frying them as an accompaniment to a meal, use them whole, dropping them straight into hot oil. If they are being soaked and ground, first cut off the stalk end and shake the chilli so that the seeds fall out. They are safe enough to handle until they have been soaked and ground, but if you handle them after this has been done, remember to wash your hands at once with soap and water.

Dried chillies, though they give plenty of heat and flavour, do not have the same volatile oils as fresh chillies and so do not have as much effect on the skin.

Rice varieties

One of the oldest grains in the world, and a staple food of more than half the world's population, rice is by far the most important item in the daily diet throughout Asia.

There are thousands of varieties. Agricultural scientists involved in producing new and higher yielding strains of rice will pick differences that are not apparent to even the most enthusiastic rice eater. But, from the Asian consumer's viewpoint, rice has qualities that a Westerner might not even notice – colour, fragrance, flavour, texture.

Rice buyers are so trained to recognise different types of rice that they can hold a few grains in the palm to warm it, sniff it through the hole made by thumb and forefinger, and know its age, variety, even perhaps where it was grown. Old rice is sought after and prized more than new rice because it tends to be fluffy and separate when cooked, even if the cook absent-mindedly adds too much water. Generally speaking, the white polished grains – whether long and fine or small and pearly (much smaller than what we know as short-grain rice) – are considered best.

The desirable features of rice are not the same in every Asian country. In China they prefer rice that is perfectly cooked but not dry and fluffy. Glossy, pearly grains are desired, each one well defined, but with a tendency to cling together so that it can easily be picked up with chopsticks. No salt is used.

Rice is sold either packaged or in bulk. Polished white rice is available as long-, medium- or short-grain. Unpolished or natural rice is available as medium- or long-grain; and in many countries it is possible to buy an aromatic table rice grown in Bangladesh, called basmati rice. In dishes where spices and flavourings are added and cooked with the rice, any type of long-grain rice may be used. In each recipe the type of rice best suited is recommended, but as a general rule, remember that medium-grain or short-grain rice gives a clinging result and long-grain rice, properly cooked, is fluffy and separate.

Preparing rice

To wash or not to wash? Among Asian cooks there will never be agreement on whether rice should be washed or not. Some favour washing the rice several times, then leaving it to soak for a while. Other good cooks insist that washing rice is stupid and wasteful, taking away what vitamins and nutrients are left after the milling process.

I have found that most rice sold in Australia does not need washing but that rice imported in bulk and packaged here picks up a lot of dust and dirt and needs thorough washing and draining.

In a recipe, if rice is to be fried before any liquid is added, the washed rice must be allowed enough time to thoroughly drain and dry, between 30 and 60 minutes. Rice to be steamed must be soaked overnight. Rice for cooking by the absorption method may be washed (or not), drained briefly and added to the pan immediately.

Cooking rice

For a fail-safe way of cooking rice perfectly every time, put the required amount of rice and water into a large saucepan with a tight-fitting lid (see the measures above right). Bring to the boil over high heat, cover, then reduce the heat to low and simmer for 20 minutes. Remove from the heat, uncover and allow the steam to escape for a few minutes before fluffing up the rice with a fork.

Transfer the rice to a serving dish with a slotted metal spoon – don't use a wooden spoon or it will crush the grains. You will notice that long-grain rice absorbs considerably more water than short-grain rice, so the two kinds are not interchangeable in recipes. Though details are given in every rice recipe, here is a general rule regarding proportions of rice and liquid.

Long-grain rice

200 g (7 oz/1 cup) rice use 500 ml
  (17 fl oz/2 cups) water

400 g (14 oz/2 cups) rice use 875 ml
  (29½ fl oz/3½ cups) water

600 g (1 lb 5 oz/3 cups) rice use
  1.25 litres (42 fl oz/5 cups) water

Use 500 ml (17 fl oz/2 cups) water for the
first cup of rice, then 375 ml (12½ fl oz/
1½ cups) water for each additional cup
of rice.

Short- or medium-grain rice

220 g (8 oz/1 cup) rice use 375 ml
  (12½ fl oz/1½ cups) water

440 g (15½ oz/2 cups) rice use 625 ml
  (21 fl oz/2½ cups) water

660 g (1 lb 7 oz/3 cups) rice use 875 ml
  (29½ fl oz/3½ cups) water

Use 375 ml (12½ fl oz/1½ cups) water
for the first cup of rice, then 250 ml
(8½ fl oz/1 cup) water for each additional
cup of rice.

Noodles

There are many different types of noodles available and different Asian countries have specific uses and preferences. Almost all of these varieties are available from large supermarkets or Asian grocery stores.

Dried egg noodles: Perhaps the most popular noodles, these are made of wheat flour. Dried egg noodles must be soaked in hot water for about 10 minutes before cooking. This is not mentioned in the cooking instructions, yet it does make cooking them so much easier – as the noodles soften the strands spread and separate and the noodles cook more evenly than when they are dropped straight into boiling water.

A spoonful of oil in the water prevents boiling over. When water returns to the boil, cook fine noodles for 2–3 minutes and thick noodles for 3–4 minutes. Do not overcook. Drain immediately, then run cold water through the noodles to rinse off any excess starch and cool them so they don't continue to cook in their own heat. Drain thoroughly. To reheat, pour boiling water over the noodles in a colander. Serve with stir-fried dishes or use in soups and braised noodle dishes.

Dried rice noodles: There are various kinds of flat rice noodles. Depending on the type of noodle and thickness of the strands, they have to be soaked in cold water for 30–60 minutes before cooking. Drain, then drop into a saucepan of boiling water and cook for 6–10 minutes, testing every minute after the first 6 minutes so you will know when they are done. As soon as they are tender, drain in a colander and rinse well in cold running water. Drain once more. They can then be fried or heated in soup before serving.

Dried rice vermicelli (rice-stick) noodles: Rice vermicelli has very fine strands and cooks very quickly. Drop into boiling water and cook for 2–3 minutes only. Drain well. Serve in soups or with dishes that have a good amount of sauce. Or, if a crisp garnish is required, use rice vermicelli straight from the packet and deep-fry small amounts for just a few seconds. It will puff and become white as soon as it is immersed in the oil if it is hot enough. Lift out quickly on a slotted spoon or wire strainer and drain on paper towels before serving.

Dried cellophane (bean thread) noodles: Also known as bean starch noodles, these dried noodles need to be soaked in hot water for 20 minutes, then drained and cooked in a saucepan of boiling water for 15 minutes, or until tender. For use as a crisp garnish, deep-fry them in hot oil straight from the packet, as for rice vermicelli (above). In Japan they have a similar fine translucent noodle, known as *harusame*.

Preparing soft-fried noodles

After the noodles have been boiled and drained, spread them on a large baking tray lined with paper towel and leave them to dry for at least 30 minutes – a little peanut oil may be sprinkled over them to prevent sticking. Heat 2 tablespoons each of peanut oil and sesame oil in a wok or large heavy-based frying pan until hot, then add a handful of noodles and cook until golden on one side. Turn and cook the other side until golden, then remove to a plate. Repeat with the remaining noodles. It may be necessary to add more oil to the wok if a large quantity of noodles is being fried, but make sure the fresh oil is very hot first. Serve with beef, pork, poultry or vegetable dishes.

Preparing crisp-fried noodles

Rice vermicelli (rice-stick) and cellophane (bean thread) noodles can be fried in hot oil straight from the packet. Egg noodles need to be cooked first, then drained and spread out on a large baking tray lined with paper towel to dry for at least 30 minutes – a little peanut oil can be sprinkled over them to prevent sticking. Heat sufficient peanut oil in a wok or heavy-based frying pan over medium heat. When the oil is hot, deep-fry the noodles, in batches, until crisp and golden brown. Drain on paper towel. These crisp noodles are used mainly as a garnish.

Preparing whole chickens

Jointing a chicken

I have often referred to cutting a chicken into serving pieces suitable for a curry. This is simply cutting the pieces smaller than joints so that the spices can more readily penetrate and flavour the meat.

To joint a chicken, first cut off the thighs and drumsticks, then separate the drumsticks from the thighs. Cut off the wings and divide them at the middle joint (wing tips may be added to a stock but do not count as a joint). The breast is divided down the centre into two, then across into four pieces – do not start cooking the breast pieces at the same time as the others, but add them later, as breast meat has a tendency to become dry if cooked for too long.

A 1.5 kg (3 lb 5 oz) chicken, for instance, can be jointed, then broken down further into serving pieces. The thighs are cut into two with a heavy cleaver; the back is cut into four pieces and used in the curry, though not counted as serving pieces because there is very little meat on them. Neck and giblets are also included to give extra flavour.

Chopping a chicken the Chinese way

After cooking, a whole chicken is divided through the centre lengthways with a sharp, heavy cleaver. Then turn each half, cut side down, on a sturdy wooden chopping board and chop crossways into 3.5 cm (1½ in) strips. Reassemble on a serving plate. If this seems a formidable task, start by cutting off the drumstick, thigh and wing. Chop each of these into two pieces. Then use the cleaver to cut the chicken through the body. With a good Chinese cleaver this is not as difficult as it sounds.

Preparing whole fish

Cutting fish fillets into serving pieces

Fish fillets are of varying thickness, length and density. For example, whole fillets of flathead can be dipped in tempura batter and will cook in less than a minute in hot oil, whereas a fillet of ling or trevalla will need to be cut into 3 cm (1¼ in) strips for the same recipe.

Let common sense prevail when portioning fish fillets, but always remember that fish is cooked when the flesh turns opaque when flaked with a fork or knife.

Cutting fish steaks into serving pieces

Depending on the size of the fish, each steak may need to be cut into four, six or eight pieces. Once again, smaller portions are better, for they allow flavours to penetrate and you can allow more than one piece per person. The accompanying sketch shows how to divide fish steaks – small ones into four pieces, medium-sized ones into six pieces and really large steaks into eight pieces.

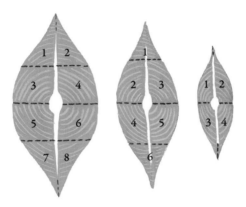

China

Imagine a visit to Hong Kong just to sample Chinese specialities and to learn from some of the best Chinese chefs in the business. I consider myself very lucky indeed to have had the chance to do just that. It was an education to see specialist chefs in action, preparing dim sum of many kinds with such speed and nimbleness of fingers that it was obvious that not just knowledge but constant practice contributed to the results.

Chefs, who specialise in noodles alone, have skills in the kitchen that are more like a magician performing sleight of hand than a chef making noodles. In seconds, lumps of well-kneaded dough were transformed into dozens of incredibly fine strands, stretched to an arm's length, the ends folded together, then stretched again so that first there was one thick rope of dough, then two, four, eight, sixteen and so on, ending in a veritable curtain of noodles which were then dropped into a bubbling cauldron.

Peking duck with mandarin pancakes was another of the famous dishes I watched being prepared with its perfectly crisp, deep reddish-brown skin. The secret is in blowing air between the skin and the flesh of the duck until it inflates like a balloon, then tying tightly around the neck and hanging it in a special drying chamber before cooking so that the skin cannot fail to achieve the right crackling crispness.

A visit to the central market in Hong Kong was enough to make my head spin, there was such variety. One can purchase anything, from dozens of different vegetables and fruits to all sorts of meat and seafood including enormous tiger prawns (shrimp), eels, snakes and live turtles. But this experience was not my first introduction to Chinese food. It has always been a part of my life.

I grew up in Eastern countries with sizable Chinese populations and the opportunity to know good Chinese food. To help matters along, the man I married is really keen on Chinese food – not just eating it, but cooking it. He would pursue recipes with the single mindedness of a bloodhound and so it came about that between us we learned a great deal about a cuisine neither of us was born into. There are many regional varieties of cooking in a country as vast as China, but there are five major styles. The Peking or Shantung style of cooking emphasises delicacy of flavour; Sichuan food is hot and spicy; Honan cooking is spicy, sweet and sour; the Fukien school of cooking is famous for its clear soups, seafood dishes and subtlety of flavouring; and Cantonese cooking, best known in Western countries, is a combination of many styles, with an emphasis on stir-fried dishes and subtle flavours, and is light and digestible because less fat is used than in other cooking styles. It is Cantonese cooking that excels in the steamed dumplings of various kinds that are known as dim sum.

The reason Cantonese food is best known abroad is because in the nineteenth century it was from Canton, in the south of China, that large numbers of Chinese emigrated to America, Europe and Southeast Asia and introduced their cooking to these regions. It became immensely popular and has remained so to this day.

A feature of Chinese food is the variety of ingredients used. This is not because the Chinese were in search of exotic foods (though in the palaces this may have been their primary aim), but because they had to be resourceful and use everything edible in order to survive. As a result, they made use of ingredients like dried wood ear fungus and lily buds (golden needles), lotus seed and lotus root, fish's maw and all kinds of meat, seafood and vegetables. Bird's nest soup is perhaps the most widely known preparation featuring an unusual ingredient. These nests are not made from twigs but from the saliva of tiny swifts and have the reputation of being very nourishing. Because the nests have to be gathered from sheer, almost inaccessible cliffs and require soaking and a lot of careful cleaning, the soup is served as a prestige course at banquets. Its presence on the menu proclaims that the host and their cooks have gone to a lot of trouble. When a special banquet is held it would not be a compliment to the guests if the menu did not include rare and expensive treats. By contrast, everyday Chinese cooking is easy and the recipes in this chapter are within the scope of the beginner cook who does not have all day to spend in the kitchen.

The cooking methods employed by the Chinese are those that are familiar in the West: boiling, braising, deep-frying, steaming and roasting. In addition, there is stir-frying, which means stirring and tossing ingredients in very little oil over high heat. It does mean that all the preparation must be done before the cooking starts, and all ingredients are cut into evenly sized pieces and shapes. The method was evolved to conserve fuel, and because of the small size of the pieces of food, the cooking time is often only 5 minutes from start to finish – a delay in preparation while ingredients are cooking could mean a disappointing result. Ingredients are added in a certain order, those which take longest to cook being put in first. With a little practice, this split-second timing becomes second nature. It is better to let guests wait for such a dish, rather than the other way around, because if the food has to wait it will continue cooking in its own heat and the effect will be spoilt. A great deal depends on texture in Chinese food and the vegetables must be crisp and the meat or fish just cooked and juicy, never overdone or dry.

Cheap cuts of lean meat, such as rump (round) steak or blade steak may be used for stir-fries, but because of the extremely short cooking time, they should be tenderised by the Chinese method. Shred or slice meat as directed. For every 500 g (1 lb 2 oz) of meat, dissolve ½ teaspoon bicarbonate of soda (baking soda) in 60 ml (2 fl oz/¼ cup) hot water. Add to the meat and knead well until the liquid is absorbed. Cover and refrigerate for 2 hours or overnight, if possible. Proceed with the recipe in the usual way. This method is used in many Chinese restaurants, making cheaper cuts of meat as tender as the choicest fillet.

Serving and eating a chinese meal

A Chinese meal does not feature one main dish, but a number of dishes of equal importance. A formal banquet is served as a succession of courses with pauses in between for drinking, conversation and playing games, which explains how diners can partake of ten or more courses. At family meals, or informal entertaining, all the dishes are placed on the table at once. This makes it unnecessary for the host to leave the table once the meal has started.

Rice is always the basis of the meal – steamed plain white rice, either short- or medium- grained, is cooked without salt. Fried rice is not usually served with meals, but is a snack in itself, composed of cold cooked rice and other ingredients. Utilising any left-over plain rice is ideal.

13

Introduction ✱

Each place-setting includes a bowl, chopsticks and porcelain spoon, cups for wine or tea and a small plate, which doubles as a saucer under the eating bowl and also as a bone plate. It is considered quite polite to extricate bones from the mouth, using chopsticks, and put them on a bone plate. A small sauce dish is also part of the individual setting for meals that require a dipping sauce.

When first choosing a menu for a Chinese meal, do not attempt more than one stir-fried dish. Instead, choose a braised dish, perhaps a cold starter, a roasted dish, soup and a cold main dish, such as chicken with oyster sauce. Desserts are not a part of Chinese meals for everyday eating, but a special meal finishes with a sweet, such as almond jelly or fresh fruit.

Utensils

A Chinese kitchen usually has a 'bench' fireplace along one wall, with holes in the bench top to hold the woks above the direct heat, most often supplied by wood fires. In restaurants they use fierce gas jets to provide the quick and flexible heat required in many Chinese cooking methods. Almost every Chinese dish can be prepared in a Western kitchen using Western equipment, but here I would urge that you acquire a wok, rather than make do with a frying pan or saucepan, because it is really a remarkably versatile utensil (see page 6).

You may use a good kitchen knife, but once you have become accustomed to a razor-sharp Chinese chopper, you'll never want to use anything else. Choppers may look clumsy with their wide blade, but the corner of the blade can do anything the point of a knife can do. A chopper is the best thing for slicing, shredding, chopping or dicing. As an extra bonus, its big blade can be used to carry cut ingredients from chopping block to cooking pan. It is wise to have both a chopper and a cleaver, the cleaver being thicker and heavier and intended for chopping through bones, a technique used widely in Chinese cooking, while the chopper with its thin blade does the more delicate jobs with ease and precision.

Use the chopper and cleaver on a wooden block or board. I do not recommend laminated chopping boards, whatever kind of knife you use – when you get down to serious cooking there's nothing to take the place of a solid wooden chopping board. Wood is safer too because the surface is not smooth and slippery.

The Chinese use steamers of bamboo and aluminium, but these are not strictly essential because it is easy enough to improvise a steamer. Steaming can be done in any covered pan large enough to accommodate a plate placed on a rack or a bowl to hold it well above the level of the boiling water. The plate should be of a size that will allow free circulation of steam around and above it. The food to be cooked is put on the plate, the pan covered with a well-fitting lid, and there you have a perfectly adequate steamer.

Chinese bamboo steamers are particularly suitable for steaming buns or dumplings, for the natural perforations of the lid allow excess steam to escape and not gather inside (as they do on a metal lid) and drop back on to the buns, making them wet and spoiling their appearance. Overcome this problem by putting buns and dim sum on a perforated rack over boiling water, cover the pan with a clean cloth folded into a double layer and then a lid. The cloth prevents steam gathering on the lid and falling back onto the buns.

Chinese ladles and frying spoons (wok chan) are useful but not strictly necessary if you have other utensils that will do the job. Any kind of ladle can be used for dipping out stock, and I have found that the curved, slotted spatula is ideal for tossing and stir-frying and for lifting food from deep oil.

Chinese skimmers, frying spoons of finely twisted wire mesh, are useful. So too is a large wire spoon that can cope with a whole fish, lifting it out of oil with ease – a consideration if you like cooking whole fish. Long wooden cooking chopsticks are also useful, especially for separating noodles as they cook, and for a variety of other purposes from beating eggs to stirring ingredients.

Fresh ingredients

In addition to the ingredients listed below, which have a long shelf life, there are the essential fresh ingredients that give flavour to Chinese food – fresh ginger, garlic, coriander (cilantro) and spring onions (scallions). When required for special dishes, fresh bean sprouts and snow peas (mangetout) can be bought and stored in the refrigerator for up to 1 week. Tofu is a popular source of protein. Chinese sausages (lap cheong) are also useful. Spring roll wrappers and won ton pastry keep well in the freezer.

Your Chinese shelf

agar-agar powder

arrowroot

baby corn

bamboo shoots, tinned

black beans, salted, tinned

chestnut flour

chestnuts, dried

chillies, large dried red

chilli oil

Chinese barbecue (char siu) sauce

Chinese chilli bean sauce

Chinese chilli sauce

Chinese five-spice

Chinese ground bean sauce

chow chow preserves (substitute ginger in syrup or bottled Sri Lankan chow chow preserve)

cornflour (cornstarch)

ginkgo nuts, tinned

hoisin sauce

lily buds (golden needles), dried

lotus nut paste, tinned

lotus root, frozen

oyster sauce

peanut oil

plum sauce

preserved melon shreds

sesame oil

sesame paste

shiitake mushrooms, dried

sichuan peppercorns

soy sauce, light, dark and mushroom

star anise

straw mushrooms, tinned

tapioca flour

walnuts

water chestnut starch

water chestnuts, tinned

wood ear fungus, dried

Rice and Noodles

*

Fan
White rice

Serves 4–6

....

500 g (1 lb 2 oz/2¼ cups) short-grain or
    medium-grain rice

Wash the rice well and drain in a colander for 30 minutes.

Put the rice and 750 ml (25½ fl oz/3 cups) water into a large saucepan and bring to the boil over high heat. Let it boil rapidly for 1–2 minutes, then reduce the heat to medium and cook until holes appear in the surface. Cover with a tight-fitting lid, reduce the heat to low and continue cooking for a further 10 minutes. Turn off the heat, without removing the lid, and let the rice sit undisturbed for a further 10 minutes to finish cooking.

Ching Choong Chow Fan
Spring onion and soy fried rice

Serves: 3–4

....

2 tablespoons peanut oil

3–4 cups cold cooked white rice (above)

1 tablespoon light soy sauce

1 tablespoon mushroom soy sauce

6 spring onions (scallions), thinly sliced

Heat the peanut oil in a wok or large heavy-based frying pan over high heat. Add the rice and stir-fry until all the grains are separate and lightly coloured. Add the sauces and toss to evenly combine, then add the spring onion and continue to toss for a further 1 minute to combine and heat through. Serve hot.

Note

You can vary this recipe to make a more elaborate fried rice so it can be a meal in its own right. Add one or more of the following ingredients, which should be stir-fried separately before combining with the rice: diced ham or bacon; diced pork; sliced Chinese sausage (lap cheong); small prawns (shrimp); beaten eggs; green peas.

Gai See Fun Guen
Steamed rice parcels

Serves: 8–10

500 g (1 lb 2 oz/2¼ cups) medium-grain rice

2 tablespoons light soy sauce

3 teaspoons sesame oil

6 dried shiitake mushrooms

1 tablespoon dark soy sauce

2 teaspoons sugar

2 boneless skinless chicken breasts, diced

250 g (9 oz) Barbecued pork (page 106), diced

1 garlic clove, crushed

½ teaspoon finely grated fresh ginger

1 teaspoon salt

2 teaspoons cornflour (cornstarch)

dried bamboo leaves or lotus leaves, rehydrated in warm water (see note)

Note

If bamboo or lotus leaves are not available, use foil to wrap the rice into secure parcels before steaming.

Put the rice and 1 litre (34 fl oz/4 cups) water into a large saucepan with the light soy sauce and 1 teaspoon of the sesame oil. Bring to the boil over high heat, then reduce the heat to low, cover, and cook for 15 minutes. Turn off the heat, without removing the lid and let the rice sit undisturbed for a further 10 minutes to finish cooking.

Meanwhile, soak the mushrooms in hot water for 20–30 minutes. Drain, reserving 310 ml (10½ fl oz/1¼ cups) of the soaking liquid, then cut off and discard the stems and thinly slice the caps.

Put the mushrooms and 190 ml (6½ fl oz/¾ cup) of the reserved soaking liquid into a large saucepan with the dark soy sauce, remaining sesame oil and the sugar. Cover and simmer over low heat for 10 minutes. Add the chicken, pork, garlic, ginger, salt and the remaining mushroom soaking liquid and mix well to combine. Re-cover and simmer for a further 5 minutes, or until the chicken is cooked through.

In a small bowl, mix together the cornflour with a little cold water to make a smooth paste. Add to the pan, stirring until the sauce turns clear, then remove from the heat and allow to cool to lukewarm.

Mix the sauce ingredients gently through the rice until well combined. Arrange four overlapping bamboo leaves or 1 lotus leaf on a clean work surface. Spoon over ¾ cup of the rice mixture and roll up into a neat parcel, securing with kitchen string. Repeat until all the rice mixture has been used – you should make about 8 parcels in total. Steam the rice parcels for 25 minutes. Serve warm or cold.

Chai Chow Fan
Vegetarian fried rice

Serves: 6

12 dried shiitake mushrooms

1 tablespoon peanut oil

1 tablespoon sesame oil

1 teaspoon finely grated fresh ginger

2 garlic cloves, finely grated

2 leeks, white part only, thinly sliced

4 celery stalks, thinly sliced

250 g (9 oz/2 cups) sliced green beans

155 g (5½ oz/1 cup) coarsely grated carrot

90 g (3 oz/1 cup) fresh bean sprouts, trimmed (optional)

250 g (9 oz/1 cup) sliced bamboo shoots (optional)

3–4 cups cold cooked white rice (page 17)

2 tablespoons light soy sauce

65 g (2¼ oz/1 cup) sliced spring onions (scallions)

Soak the mushrooms in hot water for 20–30 minutes. Drain, reserving 125 ml (4 fl oz/½ cup) of the soaking liquid, then cut off and discard the stems and thinly slice the caps.

Heat the peanut and sesame oils in a wok or large heavy-based frying pan over low heat. Add the ginger and garlic and cook for 30 seconds, then add the mushroom, leek, celery, beans and carrot and stir-fry over high heat for 3 minutes. Add the bean sprouts, if using, and bamboo shoots and stir-fry for 1 minute then add the rice and continue to stir-fry over high heat until well combined and heated through.

In a small bowl, mix together the reserved mushroom soaking liquid and soy sauce, and sprinkle evenly over the rice with the spring onion. Continue stirring to mix well together and season with salt to taste. Serve hot.

Jahp Wui Chow Min
Combination chow mein

Serves: 6

Chow mein, a popular dish in Western countries, is sometimes made with crisp fried noodles to pander to Western preference, but the authentic recipe calls for soft-fried noodles combined with other ingredients. A delicious way of using leftovers. The quantities are only a guide – use what you have on hand.

500 g (1 lb 2 oz) dried fine egg noodles

peanut oil for frying

1 garlic clove, crushed

½ teaspoon finely grated fresh ginger

175 g (6 oz/1 cup) sliced Barbecued pork (page 106)

175 g (6 oz/1 cup) diced cooked chicken

50 g (1¾ oz/½ cup) tinned abalone, sliced (optional)

75 g (2¾ oz/1 cup) shredded Chinese cabbage (wombok) or mustard cabbage (gai choy)

90 g (3 oz/1 cup) fresh bean sprouts, trimmed

8 spring onions (scallions), cut into short lengths

250 g (9 oz/1 cup) sliced bamboo shoots

2 teaspoons cornflour (cornstarch)

125 ml (4 fl oz/½ cup) light stock (page 42) or water

2 tablespoons light soy sauce

Soak the noodles in hot water for 10 minutes, then cook in a saucepan of boiling water until tender. Drain well, then soft-fry the noodles as described on page 10. Set aside and keep warm.

Heat 2 tablespoons of the peanut oil in a wok or large heavy-based frying pan over medium heat. Add the garlic and ginger and cook for a few seconds, then add the pork, chicken, abalone, cabbage, bean sprouts, spring onion and bamboo shoots and stir-fry for 1–2 minutes, or until well combined and heated through. Push the ingredients to the side of the wok.

In a small bowl, combine the cornflour and 2 tablespoons cold water and stir to make a smooth paste. Add the stock and soy sauce to the wok, bring to the boil, then stir in the cornflour mixture and continue stirring until the sauce boils and thickens. Mix in the meat and vegetables and serve immediately over the noodles.

Snacks
and
Starters

❋

Wai Tze Guen
Miniature scallop rolls

Makes: 20–24

3 dried shiitake mushrooms

185 g (6½ oz) scallops, cleaned and chopped

6 water chestnuts, roughly chopped

2 spring onions (scallions), finely chopped

½ teaspoon finely grated fresh ginger

½ teaspoon salt

1 teaspoon light soy sauce

1 teaspoon sesame oil

6 large spring roll wrappers

1 egg, lightly beaten

1½ tablespoons plain (all-purpose) flour

peanut oil for deep-frying

Soak the mushrooms in hot water for 20–30 minutes. Drain, reserving 125 ml (4 fl oz/½ cup) of the soaking liquid, then cut off and discard the stems and thinly slice the caps.

In a bowl, mix together the mushrooms, scallops, water chestnuts, spring onions, ginger, salt, soy sauce and sesame oil.

Cut each spring roll wrapper into quarters. Combine the egg and flour in a bowl and beat to a smooth, thick paste. Set aside.

Place a teaspoon of the scallop filling on each wrapper quarter, near one end. Fold the wrapper over the filling, fold in the sides and wrap up to enclose. Smear the end of the spring roll pastry with the flour paste and press gently to seal.

Heat the oil in a wok or large heavy-based frying pan over medium heat. When the oil is hot, deep-fry the rolls, in batches, for 1–2 minutes, or until golden brown all over. Drain on paper towel and serve hot.

Jar Yue Har Guen
Deep-fried fish and prawn rolls

Makes: 12

500 g (1 lb 2 oz) boneless, skinless, firm
  white fish fillets

12 raw prawns (shrimp), peeled and
  deveined

1 egg, beaten with 1 tablespoon water

½ teaspoon finely grated fresh ginger

½ teaspoon salt

plain (all-purpose) flour

dry breadcrumbs for coating

250 ml (8½ fl oz/1 cup) oil for frying

soy sauce or chilli sauce to serve

Depending on the size of the fish fillets, they may be cut into two, three or four strips – they should be thin as they need to be rolled around the prawns. Wrap each fish strip around a prawn and fasten with a wooden toothpick.

In a bowl, mix together the egg, ginger and salt. Put the flour and breadcrumbs in separate shallow bowls. Heat the oil in a wok or large heavy-based frying pan over medium heat. Dip the fish rolls first into the flour, then into the egg mixture, shaking off any excess, and finally into the breadcrumbs, turning to coat. Gently lower into the hot oil and deep-fry, in batches, for about 3 minutes, or until golden all over. Drain on paper towel. Serve hot with soy sauce or chilli sauce for dipping.

Dai Bao
Dough for steamed buns

Makes: 8–10 buns

375 g (13 oz/2½ cups) plain (all-purpose) flour

3½ teaspoons baking powder

55 g (2 oz/¼ cup) caster (superfine) sugar

2 tablespoons softened lard or butter

½ teaspoon white vinegar

sesame oil for brushing

Note

Cooked buns can be refrigerated overnight and re-heated by steaming for 3 minutes or briefly microwaving for 30 seconds before serving.

Sift the flour and baking powder into a bowl, then stir in the sugar and rub in the lard with your fingertips until evenly distributed. Combine the vinegar with 125 ml (4 fl oz/½ cup) lukewarm water, then add to the flour mixture and knead to a soft dough. Shape into a ball, cover, and rest the dough for 30 minutes.

To mould the buns, divide the dough into eight even-sized portions and shape each into a smooth ball. Use a rolling pin to roll out on a lightly floured work surface to make circles with a 10 cm (4 in) diameter, keeping the centre thicker than the edges. Cut small squares from a sheet of baking paper and brush each with a little sesame oil. Place a bun on each square of greased paper, then arrange in the top layer of a steamer.

Once you have prepared your filling, place a heaped teaspoon in the centre of each circle, gather the edges together, and fold and pleat to make a neat join, twisting to seal. Put each bun, join side down, in the steamer, cover, and steam for 20 minutes, or until well risen. Serve warm.

Cha Shiu Bao
Barbecued pork buns

Makes: 6–8 buns

2 teaspoons peanut oil

1 small garlic clove, crushed with
¼ teaspoon salt

2 teaspoons light soy sauce

½ teaspoon sesame oil, plus extra
for brushing

1 teaspoon oyster sauce

3 teaspoons cornflour (cornstarch)

1 teaspoon hoisin sauce

1 teaspoon sugar

small pinch red colouring powder (glossary)
(optional)

235 g (8½ oz/1⅓ cups) diced Barbecued
pork (page 106)

1 quantity Dough for steamed buns
(dai bao) (page 25)

Heat the peanut oil in a wok or large heavy-based frying pan over low heat. Add the garlic and cook until soft. Add the soy sauce, sesame oil, oyster sauce and 80 ml (2½ fl oz/⅓ cup) hot water.

In a small bowl, combine the cornflour and 1 tablespoon cold water and stir to make a smooth paste, then add to the wok, stirring until thick and clear. Remove from the heat, stir in the hoisin sauce, sugar and red colouring, if using. Allow to cool, then stir in the pork until well combine. Mould and steam the buns following the directions for steamed bun dough on page 25.

Ma Yung Bao
Steamed sweet bean buns

Makes: 10

These steamed buns are a snack rather than a dessert.

255 g (9 oz) tinned sweet bean paste
  (dow sah)

1 tablespoon sesame oil for brushing

1 quantity Dough for steamed buns
  (dai bao) (page 25)

Put a teaspoonful of bean paste in the centre of each circle and mould, then steam the buns following the directions for steamed bun dough on page 25. Serve warm or at room temperature.

So Jar Har Yuen
Lotus flowers

Makes: about 15

Crisp on the outside and melting soft inside, these 'lotus flowers' are served as an appetiser at a Chinese meal or as a snack.

500 g (1 lb 2 oz) raw prawns (shrimp),
  peeled, deveined and finely chopped

10 water chestnuts, finely chopped

2 spring onions (scallions), thinly sliced

½ teaspoon finely grated fresh ginger

½ teaspoon salt

1 teaspoon Chinese rice wine or dry sherry

1 egg white

1 teaspoon cornflour (cornstarch)

oil for deep-frying

In a bowl, mix together the prawn meat, water chestnuts, spring onion, ginger, salt and rice wine.

Beat the egg white until stiff, then fold through the cornflour and prawn mixture until combined. Take 1 tablespoon of the mixture at a time and roll into small balls.

Heat the oil in a wok or large heavy-based frying pan over medium heat. When the oil is hot, deep-fry the balls, in batches, for 2–3 minutes, or until golden. Drain on paper towel and serve immediately.

Woo Dip Har
Butterfly prawns

Makes: 12

12 large raw prawns (shrimp), peeled and deveined, tails left intact

1 tablespoon Chinese rice wine or dry sherry (optional)

2 tablespoons light soy sauce

1 small garlic clove, crushed with ¼ teaspoon salt

½ teaspoon finely grated fresh ginger

60 g (2 oz/½ cup) cornflour (cornstarch)

1 large egg, beaten

dry breadcrumbs for coating

peanut oil for deep-frying

Chinese chilli sauce to serve (optional)

Use a sharp knife to make a slit along the back of each prawn, being careful not to cut right through.

In a bowl, combine the rice wine, soy sauce, garlic and ginger. Add the prawns, toss to coat, then set aside to marinate for at least 15 minutes.

Put the cornflour, egg and breadcrumbs in separate shallow bowls. Heat the peanut oil in a wok or large heavy-based frying pan over medium heat. Dip the prawns first in the cornflour, then into the egg, shaking off any excess, and finally into the breadcrumbs, turning to coat. Gently lower into the hot oil and deep-fry, in batches, for 2–3 minutes, or until golden brown. Drain on paper towel and serve hot with the chilli sauce, if desired.

Har Kau or Kau Che
Prawns in translucent pastry

Makes: about 20

Filling

185 g (6½ oz) raw prawns (shrimp), peeled, deveined and chopped

2 tablespoons chopped ham or bacon fat

2 tablespoons finely chopped bamboo shoots

2 spring onions (scallions), thinly sliced

½ teaspoon finely grated fresh ginger

3 teaspoons cornflour (cornstarch)

1 teaspoon sesame oil

1 teaspoon salt

1 teaspoon sugar

Pastry

150 g (5½ oz/1 cup) plain (all-purpose) flour

60 g (2 oz/½ cup) cornflour (cornstarch)

1 tablespoon lard

sesame oil for brushing

To make the filling, combine all the ingredients in a large bowl, mixing well to combine. Set aside.

To make the pastry, mix together the flour and cornflour in a bowl. Put the lard and 250 ml (8½ fl oz/1 cup) water into a small saucepan, bring to the boil. Remove from the heat and allow to cool slightly then pour all but 2 tablespoons of the water onto the flour. Mix well and as soon as it is cool enough to handle knead to a smooth, pliable dough. Divide into two equal portions and mould each into a 12 cm (4¾ in) log, with a 3 cm (1¼ in) diameter. Wrap each log in plastic wrap to prevent the surface from drying out.

Working with one log at a time, cut into 1.5 cm (½ in) slices and flatten with a lightly greased metal spatula. Roll out to make a thin circle with a 10 cm (4 in) diameter. Put a teaspoonful of filling on each circle and fold over the pastry to make a half-moon shape, pinching the edge to seal. Brush the tops lightly with the sesame oil. Repeat with the remaining dough and filling.

Cut 10 cm (4 in) squares from a sheet of baking paper and brush with a little sesame oil. Place a pastry over each square and arrange in the top layer of a steamer basket. Steam for 12 minutes, or until translucent. Serve hot with sauces for dipping, if desired.

Snacks and Starters ❋

So Jar Gai Yuen
Golden blossoms

Makes: 12–15

250 g (9 oz) boneless skinless chicken
breast, finely chopped

250 g (9 oz) raw prawns (shrimp), peeled,
deveined and finely chopped

3 spring onions (scallions), thinly sliced

¾ teaspoon salt

2 teaspoons cornflour (cornstarch)

100 g (3½ oz/½ cup) corn kernels

2 tablespoons chopped Barbecued pork
(page 106) (optional)

1 small garlic clove, crushed

Batter

110 g (4 oz/¾ cup) plain (all-purpose) flour

1 tablespoon cornflour (cornstarch)

½ teaspoon salt

2 teaspoons peanut oil

½ teaspoon finely grated fresh ginger
(optional)

1 egg white

oi for deep-frying

To make the batter, sift the flour, cornflour and salt into
a large bowl. Add 190 ml (6½ fl oz/¾ cup) water and beat
to make a smooth batter. Stir in the peanut oil and ginger,
allow to stand for 30 minutes. Just before using, beat the egg
white until stiff and fold through.

To make the 'golden blossoms', combine all the ingredients
in a bowl. Take 1 tablespoon of the mixture at a time and
roll into balls.

Heat the oil in a wok or large heavy-based frying pan
over medium heat. Working with one ball at a time, dip
it into the batter, gently shaking off any excess and then
gently lower the balls into the hot oil. Deep-fry, in batches,
for 3–4 minutes, or until puffed and golden. Drain on paper
towel and serve hot.

If not serving immediately, heat the oil again until very
hot and re-fry the golden blossoms briefly to crisp and heat
through just before serving.

Shiu Mai
Steamed prawn dumplings

Makes: about 24

500 g (1 lb 2 oz) small raw prawns (shrimp), peeled and deveined

6 dried shiitake mushrooms

6 water chestnuts, chopped

3 tablespoons bamboo shoots, chopped

3 spring onions (scallions), chopped

250 g (9 oz) minced (ground) pork

1½ teaspoons salt

1 tablespoon light soy sauce

1 tablespoon Chinese rice wine or dry sherry (optional)

1 teaspoon sesame oil

1 egg white

150 g (5½ oz) won ton wrappers

Reserve about 24 prawns to use as a garnish and chop the remainder; set aside. Soak the mushrooms in hot water for 20–30 minutes. Drain, then cut off and discard the stems and thinly slice the caps.

In a bowl, combine the chopped prawns, mushrooms, water chestnut, bamboo shoots, spring onion, pork, salt, soy sauce, rice wine, sesame oil and egg white.

Lay the won ton wrappers out on a clean work surface. Take 1 heaped teaspoon of the prawn mixture and place in the centre of each wrapper. Gather the wrapper around the filling and press it closed to give the shape of a little money bag, open at the top. Press a prawn on top of each for decoration.

Lightly oil a steamer basket and arrange the dumplings in a single layer. Cover and steam for 20 minutes, or until cooked through. Serve hot or cold with a dipping sauce if liked.

Won Ton
Small savoury dumplings

Makes: about 40

Won tons are little squares of egg noodle dough enclosing a savoury meat mixture. They may be deep-fried and served as a crisp snack or they may be boiled in soup. Won tons are the main ingredient in 'short soup'.

6 dried shiitake mushrooms

3 tablespoons finely chopped bamboo shoots

125 g (4½ oz) raw prawn (shrimp) meat, finely chopped

4 spring onions (scallions), finely chopped

250 g (9 oz) minced (ground) pork

1½ teaspoons salt

1 tablespoon light soy sauce

1 teaspoon sesame oil

300 g (10½ oz) won ton wrappers

peanut oil for deep-frying

Soak the mushrooms in hot water for 20–30 minutes. Drain, then cut off and discard the stems and thinly slice the caps.

Blanch the bamboo shoots in a saucepan of boiling water for 1 minute, then drain.

In a bowl, combine the mushroom, bamboo shoots, prawn meat, spring onion, pork, salt, soy sauce and sesame oil.

Lay the won ton wrappers out on a clean work surface. Take 1 heaped teaspoon of the prawn mixture and place in the centre of each wrapper. Moisten the edges of the dough with water, fold over to make a triangle with points crossing rather than lined up and press together firmly. Then bring the two ends together, dab with a little of the filling mixture where they join and press to seal.

Heat the peanut oil in a wok or large heavy-based frying pan over medium heat. Gently lower the won tons into the hot oil and deep-fry, in batches, for about 2 minutes, or until golden. Serve as an appetiser or as part of a meal with Sweet sour sauce (page 137).

Chai Dim Sum
Vegetarian dim sum

Makes: about 36

300 g (10½ oz/2 cups) gluten flour

6 dried shiitake mushrooms

60 ml (2 fl oz/¼ cup) peanut oil

2 spring onions (scallions), thinly sliced

1 garlic clove, crushed

1 teaspoon finely grated fresh ginger

150 g (5½ oz/2 cups) shredded cabbage

100 g (3½ oz/½ cup) finely chopped
  bamboo shoots or water chestnuts

2 tablespoons light soy sauce

2 teaspoons sesame oil

3 teaspoons salt

2 tablespoons cornflour (cornstarch)

2 eggs, lightly beaten

300 g (10½ oz) won ton wrappers

Put the gluten flour and water into a large mixing bowl and stir well, then knead until smooth. Set aside for 1 hour. Put 2 litres (68 fl oz/8 cups) water into a saucepan and bring to the boil, then cut walnut-sized pieces of dough, drop into the water and simmer for 30 minutes, or until the dough rises to the surface. Drain well, allow to cool, then chop or mince (grind) finely. Set aside.

Soak the mushrooms in hot water for 20–30 minutes. Drain, then cut off and discard the stems and thinly slice the caps.

Heat the peanut oil in a wok or large heavy-based frying pan over low heat. Add the spring onion, garlic and ginger and cook for 2 minutes, then add the cabbage and stir-fry until soft. Add the bamboo shoots, mushroom, minced gluten dough and stir-fry for 1–2 minutes. Remove from the heat, put into a large bowl and add the soy sauce, sesame oil, salt, cornflour and enough beaten egg to bind the mixture together.

Take a won ton wrapper in the palm of your hand. Put a tablespoonful of mixture in the centre and gather up the pastry to enclose the filling. With the back of a teaspoon, press points of the dough down to cover. Squeeze the dumpling firmly to make the dough adhere to the filling. Put in an oiled steamer and steam for 10 minutes. Serve hot.

Doong Gwoo Lap Cheong Jing Ju Yook
Mushroom, pork and chicken sausage

Serves: 8–10

8 dried shiitake mushrooms

500 g (1 lb 2 oz) boneless skinless chicken breasts, diced

125 g (4½ oz) Barbecued pork (page 106), diced

100 g (3½ oz) tinned bamboo shoots or water chestnuts, finely chopped

1 large garlic clove, crushed with 1 teaspoon salt

½ teaspoon finely grated fresh ginger

2 tablespoons light soy sauce

1 tablespoon Chinese rice wine or dry sherry

¼ teaspoon freshly ground pepper

1 teaspoon sugar

3 teaspoons cornflour (cornstarch)

1 tablespoon sesame oil

1 tablespoon Chinese barbecue (char siu) sauce

1 large length of sausage skin (see note)

Preheat the oven to 170°C (340°F). Soak the mushrooms in hot water for 20–30 minutes. Drain, then cut off and discard the stems and thinly slice the caps.

In a bowl, combine all the ingredients, except the sausage skin, and mix well.

Using a funnel, push the chicken mixture into the sausage skin. Tie a knot in the skin about 1 metre (40 in) from the beginning. When you have filled the skin, you will have a sausage, which you need to coil around and put on a wire rack. Prick the sausage with a very fine sharp skewer to prevent it from bursting. Put the rack over a roasting tray with 2 cm (¾ in) hot water in it. Roast in the oven for 25 minutes, then turn and roast for a further 25 minutes, or until brown. Cut into short lengths to serve.

Note

When buying the sausage skin from your butcher, emphasise that you need the large one. (My butcher once gave me the small size by mistake, and you should have seen the fun I had getting the filling in!) The skin should be thoroughly cleaned and ready for use, but if liked, soak it in salted water at home while preparing the filling, then fit one end of it on the cold water tap and run water through it.

Lahng Poon
Cold hors d'oeuvre

Serves: 6–8

If tinned abalone is unavailable, use frozen. Thaw partially and slice while still semi-frozen.

455 g (15½ oz) tinned abalone, rinsed, drained and thinly sliced

2 dried Chinese sausages (lap cheong)

½ quantity Braised mushrooms (page 124), thinly sliced

200 g (7 oz) Barbecued pork (page 106), thinly sliced

1 cooked boneless skinless chicken breast, thinly sliced

6 Tea eggs (page 38), quartered

1 large cucumber, thinly sliced

1 daikon (white radish), thinly sliced

Marinade

80 ml (2½ fl oz/⅓ cup) light soy sauce

1 tablespoon sugar

1 tablespoon Chinese rice wine or dry sherry

1 tablespoon sesame oil

½ teaspoon finely grated fresh ginger

To make the marinade, combine all the ingredients in a bowl and stir well to combine.

Put the abalone into the marinade and toss to coat, then set aside to marinate for 2 hours. (If using fresh abalone, cook briefly in a steamer for 5 minutes before marinating.)

Steam the sausages for 10 minutes, or until plump. Allow to cool and then thinly slice diagonally.

Drain the abalone and reserve the marinade.

To serve, arrange the ingredients on a large serving plate and serve the marinade in a small bowl as a dip.

Pok Pang
Mandarin pancakes

Makes: 20 pancakes to serve 4–5

These delicate crêpes are traditionally served with Peking duck, but are also used to enclose a variety of fillings such as egg foo yong, shredded pork or chicken. The filling is seasoned with a dab of rich-flavoured sauce, sprinkled with finely shredded spring onion (scallion), then rolled up and eaten as a snack.

300 g (10½ oz/2 cups) plain (all-purpose) flour

190 ml (6½ fl oz/¾ cup) boiling water

1 tablespoon sesame oil

Put the flour into a large bowl and pour over the boiling water, stirring with chopsticks or the handle of a wooden spoon for a few minutes. As soon as it is cool enough to handle, knead for 10 minutes to make a smooth, soft dough. Put the dough on a chopping board, cover with a bowl, and stand for at least 30 minutes.

Roll the dough into a log and cut into 10 even-sized slices. Keep covered with plastic wrap to prevent it from drying out. Take one slice at a time and cut it into two equal pieces. Roll each to a smooth ball, then use a rolling pin to roll out on a lightly floured work surface to make circles with an 8 cm (3¼ in) diameter. Brush one circle lightly with sesame oil, taking it right to the edge of the circle. Place a second circle on top of the first one and roll out again, to make one thin, larger circle with an 18 cm (7 in) diameter. Cover with plastic wrap while rolling the remaining dough.

Heat a large heavy-based frying pan or griddle plate over low heat. Dry-fry the pancakes, one at a time, until small bubbles develop on the surface, then turn to cook on the other side – a few golden spots will appear.

Remove from the pan and gently pull the two circles apart – the sesame oil they were brushed with makes this quite easy. Pile the pancakes on a plate and cover tightly or they will dry out. The pancakes should be soft and pliable, not brittle. To serve, fold each pancake into quarters.

To re-heat, arrange the pancakes in a steamer lined with a clean tea towel (dish towel), cover, and put over simmering water for 1–2 minutes until heated through.

Snacks and Starters ✿

Cha Yip Dahn
Tea eggs or marbled eggs

Makes: 6

6 eggs

3 tablespoons black tea leaves

1 tablespoon salt

1 tablespoon Chinese five-spice

Put the eggs and 1 litre (34 fl oz/4 cups) water into a large saucepan and bring to the boil, stirring gently (this helps to centre the yolks). Reduce the heat to low and simmer gently for 7 minutes. Cool the eggs under cold running water for 5 minutes. Lightly crack each egg shell by rolling on a hard surface – the shell should be cracked all over, but still intact (do not remove).

Put 1 litre (34 fl oz/4 cups) water into a saucepan and bring to the boil. Add the tea leaves, salt and five-spice, then add the cracked eggs. Reduce the heat to low, cover, and simmer for about 30 minutes, or until the shells turn brown. Remove from the heat and let the eggs stand in the covered pan for 30 minutes longer (or overnight if possible). Drain, cool and peel. The peeled eggs will have a marbled pattern on them. Cut into quarters and serve with a dipping sauce.

So Jar For Tui Gai Guen
Chicken and ham rolls

Serves: 4–8

....

4 boneless skinless chicken breasts

1.5 cm (½ in) thick slice ham

1 teaspoon salt

¼ teaspoon freshly ground black pepper

¼ teaspoon Chinese five-spice

1 small garlic clove, crushed

2 eggs, beaten

2 tablespoons plain (all-purpose) flour

4 spring roll wrappers

oil for deep-frying

Sauce

70 g (2½ oz/¼ cup) chopped mixed Chinese
 pickles, plus 125 ml (4 fl oz/½ cup) syrup

1 tablespoon tomato sauce (ketchup)

2 tablespoons sugar

1–2 tablespoons white vinegar

¼ teaspoon salt

2 teaspoons arrowroot

Put the chicken breasts between two sheets of baking paper and pound using a meat mallet until thin. Cut the ham into 1.5 cm (½ in) strips, the same length as the chicken.

In a bowl, combine the salt, pepper, five-spice and the garlic and smear each piece of chicken with a mere trace of the mixture. Put a length of ham on each piece of chicken and roll up, covering the ham completely and moulding the chicken flesh to seal it in.

Season the egg with ½ teaspoon of the remaining spice mixture. Put the flour in a separate bowl. Lay out the spring roll wrappers. Working with one roll of chicken at a time, dip it first in the egg and then in the flour, to coat. Place diagonally on top of a spring roll wrapper, roll over twice, then fold in the ends to enclose the chicken. Brush the ends with a little beaten egg mixed to a thick paste with flour, and use to seal the ends of the rolls.

Heat the oil in a wok or large heavy-based frying pan over medium heat. When the oil is hot, deep-fry the rolls for 3–4 minutes each, turning them so they brown evenly. Drain on paper towel. Serve hot, with the sauce on the side.

To make the sauce, put the pickle liquid, tomato sauce, sugar, vinegar, salt and 125 ml (4 fl oz/½ cup) water into a saucepan. Bring to the boil, stirring to dissolve the sugar. Combine the arrowroot and 1 tablespoon water to make a smooth paste then add to the pan with the pickles and bring to the boil, stirring until the sauce clears and thickens.

Note

For some people this dish wouldn't seem authentic without the vivid red of the dipping sauce. If this is the case, use a pinch or a few drops of red food colouring instead of the tomato sauce.

Soups

*

Yue Sheung Tong
Basic fish stock

Makes: 1 litre (34 fl oz/4 cups)

....

750 g (1 lb 11 oz) fish heads and trimmings or prawn (shrimp) heads and shells

10 whole black peppercorns

3 slices fresh ginger

1 carrot

2 celery stalks

1 large onion

2 fresh coriander (cilantro) leaves and stems

Wash the fish trimmings or prawn heads and shells. Put into a large saucepan with all the remaining ingredients and 2 litres (68 fl oz/8 cups) water and bring to the boil. Reduce the heat to low, cover, and simmer for 1 hour. Strain the stock before using. This stock can be stored in an airtight container in the refrigerator for up to 3 days or frozen for up to 4 months.

Gai Sheung Tong
Basic chicken stock

Makes: 1 litre (34 fl oz/4 cups)

....

2 kg (4 lb 6 oz) chicken bones and trimmings

10 whole black peppercorns

2 small celery stalks with leaves

1 onion

3–4 fresh coriander (cilantro) leaves and stems

2 slices fresh ginger

salt to taste

Put the chicken and all the remaining ingredients into a large saucepan with 2 litres (68 fl oz/8 cups) water and bring to the boil. Reduce the heat to low, cover, and simmer for 45–60 minutes, skimming off any scum that rises to the surface. Strain, discarding the solids, and use as directed. If the stock is fatty, chill until the fat congeals, lift off and discard. This stock can be stored in an airtight container in the refrigerator for up to 3 days or frozen for up to 4 months.

Ju Yook Sheung Tong
Basic pork stock

Makes: 1 litre (34 fl oz/4 cups)

500 g (1 lb 2 oz) pork bones

3 slices fresh ginger

¼ teaspoon whole black peppercorns

1 onion or 2 spring onions (scallions)

1 celery stalk with leaves

1 carrot

3–4 fresh coriander (cilantro) leaves and stems

light soy sauce and salt to taste

Put the pork bones and 2–2.5 litres (68–85 fl oz/8–10 cups) water into a large saucepan and bring to the boil. Reduce the heat to low and simmer, skimming off any scum that rises to the surface. Add the ginger, peppercorns, onion, celery, carrot and coriander, cover, and continue to simmer for 2 hours or longer. Add the soy sauce and salt to taste, then remove from the heat and allow to cool. Strain, discarding the solids. Refrigerate the stock and when chilled remove the fat that congeals on the surface before using. This stock can be stored in an airtight container in the refrigerator for up to 3 days or frozen for up to 4 months.

Ngau Yook Sheung Tong
Basic beef stock

Makes: 1 litre (34 fl oz/4 cups)

1 kg (2 lb 3 oz) soup (beef) bones

500 g (1 lb 2 oz) stewing steak

1 onion

1 celery stalk with leaves

1 whole star anise

4 fresh coriander (cilantro) or parsley sprigs

3 teaspoons salt

Put the bones and beef in a large saucepan with all the remaining ingredients and 2 litres (68 fl oz/8 cups) water and bring to the boil. Reduce the heat to low, cover, and simmer for 2 hours. Strain and allow to cool, then chill. Refrigerate the stock and when chilled remove the fat that congeals on the surface before using. This stock can be stored in an airtight container in the refrigerator for up to 3 days or frozen for up to 4 months.

Yue Tong Min
Fish soup with noodles

Serves: 5–6

1 tablespoon peanut oil

1 garlic clove, crushed

1 teaspoon finely chopped fresh ginger

1.5 litres (51 fl oz/6 cups) Fish stock (page 42)

500 g (1 lb 2 oz) skinless, boneless, firm
   white fish fillets, cut into bite-sized pieces

90–135 g (3–5 oz) dried egg noodles,
   cooked, or 500 g (1 lb 2 oz) fresh egg
   noodles

a few drops of sesame oil

2 tablespoons chopped fresh coriander
   (cilantro) leaves

Heat the peanut oil in a saucepan over low heat. Add the garlic and ginger and cook for a few seconds. Add the fish stock and bring to the boil. Add the fish and boil for 5 minutes, then add the noodles and bring back to the boil. Stir in the sesame oil and serve immediately, garnished with the coriander.

Ju Yook Har Kau Doong Shun Tong
Pork and prawn ball soup

Serves: 6

Pork balls

500 g (1 lb 2 oz) minced (ground) pork

1 teaspoon finely grated fresh ginger

1 garlic clove, crushed

1 teaspoon salt

2 tablespoons finely chopped spring onions
(scallions)

Prawn balls

500 g (1 lb 2 oz) raw prawns (shrimp),
peeled, deveined and finely chopped

¼ teaspoon finely grated fresh ginger

½ teaspoon salt

1 slice soft white bread, crumbled

1 egg yolk

1 teaspoon cornflour (cornstarch)

Soup

1.5 litres (51 fl oz/6 cups) Pork or Chicken
stock (page 43 or page 42)

1 tablespoon Chinese rice wine or dry
sherry

3 tablespoons tinned bamboo shoots, sliced

3 teaspoons cornflour (cornstarch)

½ teaspoon sesame oil

2 tablespoons finely chopped spring onion
(scallion) to garnish

To make the pork balls, combine all the ingredients in a bowl. Take 1 tablespoon of the mixture at a time and roll into balls.

To make the prawn balls, combine all the ingredients in a bowl. Take 1 tablespoon of the mixture at a time and roll into balls.

Drop the pork balls into the simmering stock and cook for 15 minutes. Return to simmering point, drop in the prawn balls and cook for a further 7 minutes. Remove pork and prawn balls, using a slotted spoon and set aside.

Add the rice wine and bamboo shoots to the simmering stock. Combine the cornflour and 2 tablespoons cold water in a bowl to make a smooth paste, then add to the stock, stirring until the soup is clear and thickened. Stir in the sesame oil. Return the pork and prawn balls to the soup and serve, garnished with the spring onion.

Wong Nga Bahk Tong
Pale green soup

Serves: 4–5

1 tablespoon peanut oil

½ teaspoon finely grated fresh ginger

1 garlic clove, crushed

1.25 litres (42 fl oz/5 cups) hot Chicken stock (page 42)

185 g (6½ oz/1 cup) cold cooked white rice (page 17)

750 g (1 lb 11 oz) Chinese cabbage (wombok), finely shredded

4 spring onions (scallions), thinly sliced, plus extra to garnish

1 tablespoon Chinese rice wine or dry sherry

½ teaspoon sesame oil

Heat the peanut oil in a large heavy-based saucepan over low heat. Add the ginger and garlic and cook for 1 minute. Add the hot stock and rice and simmer for 30 minutes, or until the rice is very soft. Add the cabbage and spring onion and bring to the boil, then reduce the heat to low and simmer for 5–7 minutes – the spring onion will be bright green when they first come to the boil, then cook to a paler shade of green. At this point stir in the rice wine and sesame oil, and serve immediately, garnished with the extra spring onion.

Gay Lim Sook Mi Gai Tong
Chicken velvet and sweet corn soup

Serves: 4–5

Chicken velvet is the name given to a purée made from chicken meat (usually breast meat) and egg white. This is minced (ground) or very finely chopped so it is smooth in texture. The delicate golden soup combines the purée with creamed corn.

1 large boneless skinless chicken breast

½ teaspoon salt

2 egg whites, beaten until frothy

1.25 litres (42 fl oz/5 cups) Chicken stock (page 42)

1½ tablespoons cornflour (cornstarch)

250 g (9 oz/1 cup) tinned creamed corn

1 teaspoon sesame oil

2 tablespoons Chinese rice wine or dry sherry

2 thin slices smoked ham or bacon, finely chopped

To make the chicken velvet, chop the chicken very finely until it is almost a paste. Place in a large bowl, add the salt and 2 tablespoons water and mix well to combine. Fold in the egg white to combine.

Put the chicken stock into a large saucepan and bring to the boil. Combine the cornflour and 1 tablespoon cold water in a small bowl to make a smooth paste and add to the pan with the corn. Bring back to the boil and cook until thickened, about 1 minute. Stir in the sesame oil, rice wine and the chicken velvet. Reduce the heat to low, stir well, and simmer for 2–3 minutes. Serve immediately, garnished with the ham.

Chang Dau Ngau Yook See Tong
Shredded beef and green pea soup

Serves: 4–5

250 g (9 oz) lean beef

½ teaspoon salt

1 whole star anise

1 teaspoon finely chopped fresh ginger

1 tablespoon Chinese rice wine or dry sherry

310 g (11 oz/2 cups) frozen peas

2 teaspoons cornflour (cornstarch)

2 eggs, lightly beaten

4 spring onions (scallions), thinly sliced, to garnish

Cut the beef into thin slices, then into shreds – thin slices are easier to achieve if the meat is partially frozen.

Put the beef, salt, star anise, ginger, rice wine and 1.25 litres (42 fl oz/5 cups) water into a large saucepan and bring to the boil. Reduce the heat to low, cover, and simmer for 15 minutes. Add the peas, and cook for 5 minutes. Discard the star anise.

In a small bowl, combine the cornflour and 1 tablespoon cold water to make a smooth paste and stir into the soup.

When the soup boils, stop stirring, dribble in the egg and cook for a further 1 minute. Season with salt, if needed. Serve immediately, garnished with the spring onion.

Jahp Wui Tong Min
Combination long soup

Serves: 6

6 dried shiitake mushrooms

2 eggs, beaten

2 teaspoons sesame oil

250 g (9 oz) fine egg noodles

2 litres (68 fl oz/8 cups) hot Chicken stock
(page 42)

2 tablespoons peanut oil

1 garlic clove, bruised

2 slices fresh ginger

250 g (9 oz) lean pork or chicken, finely
chopped

225 g (8 oz/3 cups) shredded Chinese
cabbage (wombok)

250 g (9 oz/1 cup) tinned bamboo shoots,
diced

2 tablespoons light soy sauce

2 tablespoons Chinese rice wine or dry
sherry

Soak the mushrooms in hot water for 20–30 minutes. Drain, then cut off and discard the stems and thinly slice the caps.

Season the egg with a little salt and freshly ground black pepper. Heat 1 teaspoon of the sesame oil in an omelette pan over low heat. Add half the egg to make a thin omelette, folding once cooked. Repeat with the remaining egg. Thinly slice the omelettes and set aside.

Cook the noodles in a saucepan of boiling water until tender. Drain well. Put the stock into a large saucepan and bring to a simmer.

Heat the peanut oil in a wok or large heavy-based frying pan. Add the garlic and ginger and cook until brown, then remove with a slotted spoon. Add the pork to the flavoured oil and cook until it changes colour. Add the cabbage and bamboo shoots and stir-fry for 2 minutes.

Add the fried mixture and noodles to the simmering chicken stock and bring to the boil. Add the soy sauce, rice wine and salt to taste. Stir in the remaining sesame oil and serve immediately, garnished with the omelette strips.

Sze Chuen Tong
Sichuan soup

Serves: 6–8

15 dried shiitake mushrooms

1 tablespoon oil

100 g (3½ oz/½ cup) finely chopped
Barbecued pork (page 106)

1 tablespoon dark soy sauce

2 teaspoons sugar

100 g (3½ oz) chopped cooked prawns
(shrimp)

95 g (3¼ oz/½ cup) diced fresh tofu

1.5 litres (51 fl oz/6 cups) Chicken or Pork
stock (page 42 or page 43)

90 g (3 oz) cellophane (bean thread)
noodles, soaked in hot water for
20 minutes, drained and cut into
short lengths

1 tablespoon light soy sauce

1 tablespoon Chinese sweet vinegar or
other mild vinegar

1 tablespoon Chinese rice wine or dry
sherry

1 teaspoon chilli oil

2 eggs, lightly beaten

1½ tablespoons cornflour (cornstarch)

1 tablespoon dried wood ear fungus,
soaked in hot water for 10 minutes, then
drained and finely chopped

Soak the mushrooms in hot water for 20–30 minutes.
Drain, then cut off and discard the stems and thinly slice the
caps. Set aside.

Heat the oil in a large saucepan over medium heat. Add the
mushroom and pork, stirring constantly, until they start
to turn brown. Add the dark soy sauce, sugar and 60 ml
(2 fl oz/¼ cup) water, cover, and simmer until all the liquid
is absorbed. Add the prawn meat and tofu and stir-fry for
1 minute, then add the stock and noodles, bring to the boil,
then reduce the heat and simmer for 3 minutes. Add the
light soy sauce, vinegar, rice wine and chilli oil. Dribble the
egg into the simmering soup, stirring constantly so that the
egg sets into fine shreds. In a small bowl, mix the cornflour
with 60 ml (2 fl oz/¼ cup) cold water to make a smooth
paste, then add to the soup away from the heat. Return to
the heat and stir constantly until the soup thickens. Season
with salt and freshly ground black pepper to taste.

Put a spoonful of wood ear fungus in the bottom of each
soup bowl and pour over the boiling soup. Serve immediately.

Suan-La Tang
Sichuan hot and sour soup

Serves: 6

60 g (2 oz) cellophane (bean thread) noodles

4 dried shiitake mushrooms

1.5 litres (51 fl oz/6 cups) Pork or Chicken stock (page 43 or page 42)

175 g (6 oz/1 cup) finely chopped cooked pork or chicken, or a mixture of both

1 tinned bamboo shoot, chopped

1 teaspoon finely grated fresh ginger

1 tablespoon cornflour (cornstarch)

1 egg, lightly beaten

1–2 tablespoons tomato sauce (ketchup)

1 tablespoon light soy sauce

½ teaspoon salt, or to taste

1 tablespoon vinegar

freshly ground black pepper to taste

a pinch of chilli powder (optional)

2 teaspoons sesame oil

2 spring onions (scallions), thinly sliced

Soak the noodles in hot water for 20 minutes, the drain well and cut into short lengths. Soak the mushrooms in hot water for 20–30 minutes. Drain, then cut off and discard the stems and thinly slice the caps.

Put the stock into a large saucepan with the noodles, mushroom, pork, bamboo shoot and ginger. Bring to the boil. In a small bowl, combine the cornflour and 60 ml (2 fl oz/¼ cup) cold water to make a smooth paste. Add to the simmering soup, stirring constantly until it boils and clears. Dribble the egg into the soup, stirring rapidly with chopsticks or a fork so that it sets in fine shreds.

Remove the soup from the heat, add the remaining ingredients and mix well to combine, Taste and adjust the seasoning as required – the taste should be quite sour and hot, but not overpoweringly so.

Dahn Far Tong
Egg flower soup

Serves: 4–5

This simple, nourishing soup can be made in a few minutes, using chicken stock. The beaten egg will set when poured into the boiling soup and look like chrysanthemum petals.

1 litre (34 fl oz/4 cups) Chicken stock (page 42)

2 tablespoons Chinese rice wine or dry sherry

1 teaspoon sesame oil

3 eggs, lightly beaten

3 tablespoons thinly sliced spring onion (scallion) to garnish

Put the stock into a large saucepan and bring to the boil. Add the rice wine and sesame oil. Taste and add salt, if needed.

Season the egg with salt. Dribble the egg into the soup, stirring rapidly with chopsticks or a fork so that it sets in fine shreds. Serve immediately, garnished with the spring onion.

Hai Yook Dahn Gung
Crab and egg soup

Serves: 5–6

I recall a Chinese restaurant in Colombo that specialised in this soup. Their chef made it with fresh crab and it was a soup to remember. But tinned or frozen crabmeat may be substituted if fresh crab is difficult to obtain.

1.5 litres (51 fl oz/6 cups) Fish or Chicken stock (page 42)

4 eggs, lightly beaten

2 tablespoons cornflour (cornstarch)

350 g (12½ oz/2 cups) crabmeat

6 spring onions (scallions), thinly sliced

Put the stock into a large saucepan and bring to the boil. Dribble the egg into the soup, stirring rapidly with chopsticks or a fork so that it sets in fine shreds.

Combine the cornflour and 80 ml (2½ fl oz/⅓ cup) water in a small bowl to make a smooth paste. Add it to the simmering stock, bring to the boil and stir constantly until it is clear and slightly thickened.

Add the crabmeat and stir to combine and heat through. Serve immediately, garnished with the spring onion.

Seafood

✻

Choy Yuen Har Kau Chow Mi Fun

Rice vermicelli with prawns and Chinese cabbage

Serves: 3–4

250 g (9 oz) rice vermicelli (rice-stick)
   noodles

1 garlic clove, crushed

1 teaspoon finely grated fresh ginger

1 tablespoon Chinese rice wine or dry
   sherry

1 teaspoon salt

1 tablespoon light soy sauce

125 ml (4 fl oz/½ cup) Fish or
   Chicken stock (page 42)

1 tablespoon peanut oil

250 g (9 oz) raw prawns (shrimp), peeled
   and deveined

6 leaves Chinese cabbage (wombok) or
   mustard cabbage (gai choy), thinly sliced

Soak the rice vermicelli noodles according to the packet instructions.

In a bowl, mix together the garlic, ginger, rice wine, salt, soy sauce and stock until well combined.

Heat the peanut oil in a wok or large heavy-based frying pan over high heat. Add the prawns and stir-fry until they change colour, then remove to a plate.

Add the cabbage to the wok and stir-fry for 1 minute, then add the combined stock mixture and cook for a further 2 minutes. Add the rice vermicelli to the wok and toss until heated through, then return the prawns to the wok, toss and serve immediately.

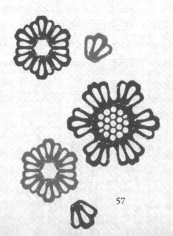

Yau Pao Yiu Gor Yue Kow
Quick boiled fish with fried cashew nuts

Serves: 4–6

....

1.5 kg (3 lb 5 oz) whole snapper or other
 firm white fish

1 large onion, thinly sliced

2 celery stalks with leaves

1 large carrot, quartered

6 thin slices fresh ginger

125 ml (4 fl oz/½ cup) Chinese rice wine or
 dry sherry

½ teaspoon whole black peppercorns

2 chicken stock (bouillon) cubes

For dressing fish

60 ml (2 fl oz/¼ cup) oil

80 g (2¾ oz/½ cup) cashew nuts, toasted

125 g (4½ oz/½ cup) Barbecued pork
 (page 106), diced

1 tablespoon dark soy sauce

2 teaspoons sesame oil

2 spring onions (scallions), thinly sliced

Clean and scale the fish, leaving the head on. Wipe inside the fish cavity with damp paper towel that has first been dipped in coarse salt. Trim any long spines or fins neatly.

Pour enough water into a wok or large heavy-based frying pan to cover the fish, but don't add the fish yet. Add all the other ingredients and bring to the boil. Reduce the heat to low and allow to simmer for 5 minutes, then bring to a fast boil and add the fish. After the water comes to the boil again, reduce the heat to low and poach the fish for 8–10 minutes, or until cooked through. Turn off the heat, carefully lift out the fish and allow any excess liquid to drain off, then put the fish on a serving platter.

To dress the fish, heat the oil in a wok over medium heat. Add the cashew nuts and stir until golden, then remove to a plate and reserve the oil. Add the pork to the wok and stir-fry until crisp. Pour off the fat that has collected in the wok, return 3 tablespoons of oil in which the cashew nuts were fried and heat gently. Combine the soy sauce and sesame oil and spoon over the fish, then quickly pour over the hot oil. Garnish with the spring onion, pork and cashew nuts before serving.

Ho Nam Jum Choa Yue
Boiled whole snapper, Honan-style

Serves: 4

750 g (1 lb 11 oz) whole snapper or other firm white fish

2 teaspoons salt

2 tablespoons peanut oil

1 teaspoon finely grated fresh ginger

8 spring onions (scallions), thinly sliced

2 teaspoons sesame oil

2 tablespoons light soy sauce

Clean and scale the fish, leaving the head on. Wipe inside the fish cavity with damp paper towel that has first been dipped in coarse salt. Trim any long spines or fins neatly.

Pour enough water into a wok or large heavy-based frying pan to cover the fish, but don't add the fish yet. Add the salt and bring to the boil. Gently lower the fish into the wok, cover, then reduce the heat to low and poach for 5–7 minutes. Remove from the wok using a slotted spoon and drain well.

Heat the peanut oil in a small saucepan over low heat. Add the ginger and spring onion and cook until soft but not brown. Remove from the heat and stir in the sesame oil and soy sauce.

Arrange the fish on a serving dish, spoon the sauce over the top and serve immediately.

Hung Shiu Yue Har Guen
Braised fish and prawn rolls

Serves: 4–6

750 g (1 lb 11 oz) skinless, boneless, firm white fish fillets

18 raw prawns (shrimp), peeled and deveined

2 tablespoons peanut oil

3 thin slices fresh ginger

1½ tablespoons light soy sauce

2 tablespoons Chinese rice wine or dry sherry

½ teaspoon sugar

1 teaspoon cornflour (cornstarch) or arrowroot

1 spring onion (scallion), thinly sliced

Wipe the fish with damp paper towel. Cut the fish into 18 strips, each large enough to roll around a prawn. Place a prawn in the centre of each strip and roll up to enclose, securing each roll with a toothpick.

Heat the peanut oil in a wok or large heavy-based frying pan over low heat. Add the ginger and cook until golden. Add the fish and prawn rolls and cook for 2 minutes, turning carefully halfway through. Add the soy sauce, rice wine, sugar and 190 ml (6½ fl oz/¾ cup) hot water to the wok, cover, and simmer for 5 minutes, or until done. Remove the fish rolls to a serving dish using a slotted spoon.

In a small bowl, combine the cornflour and 1 tablespoon water to make a smooth paste. Add to the wok with the spring onion, stirring until the sauce boils and thickens. Remove and discard the ginger, then pour the hot sauce over the fish. Serve with rice or noodles.

Suen Laht Cheung Boon Yue
Deep-fried fish with hot sour sauce

Serves: 4

500 g (1 lb 2 oz) skinless, boneless, firm
  white fish fillets

½ teaspoon salt

½ teaspoon finely grated fresh ginger

1 egg white, lightly beaten

oil for frying

cornflour (cornstarch) for dusting

Sauce

140 g (5 oz/½ cup) tinned Chinese mixed
  pickles, thinly sliced, plus 125 ml (4 fl oz/
  ½ cup) liquid

1 tablespoon sugar

½ teaspoon salt

1 tablespoon cornflour (cornstarch)

1 fresh red chilli, deseeded and thinly sliced

1 fresh green chilli, deseeded and thinly
  sliced

Wipe the fish with damp paper towel. Cut the fish into
serving portions (see page 11). Sprinkle over the salt and rub
over the fresh ginger, then pour over the egg white and turn
to coat both sides. Set aside while preparing the sauce.

To make the sauce, put the pickle liquid, sugar, salt and
125 ml (4 fl oz/½ cup) water into a small saucepan and bring
to the boil. Combine the cornflour and 60 ml (2 fl oz/¼ cup)
water in a separate bowl to make a smooth paste, then stir
into the pan until thickened and clear. Stir in the pickles and
chilli. Set aside and keep warm until ready to serve.

Heat the oil in a wok or large heavy-based frying pan over
medium heat. Toss the fish pieces in cornflour to coat then
deep-fry the fish for 3–4 minutes, or until golden – do not
overcook the fish or it will become dry. Drain on paper
towel. Arrange the fish on a serving platter, pour the hot
sauce over the top and serve immediately with rice.

Sze Chuen Yau Jar Yue
Deep-fried fish, Sichuan-style

Serves: 4

4 × 375 g (13 oz) whole firm white fish

2 tablespoons Chinese rice wine or dry sherry

2 tablespoons light soy sauce

2 teaspoons cornflour (cornstarch)

2 tablespoons dark soy sauce

1 teaspoon sugar

oil for frying

1 tablespoon finely grated fresh ginger

5 garlic cloves, finely chopped

2 tablespoons Chinese chilli bean sauce

4 spring onions (scallions), thinly sliced

Clean and scale the fish, leaving the head on. Wipe inside the fish cavity with damp paper towel that has first been dipped in coarse salt. Trim any long spines or fins neatly. With a sharp knife score vertical cuts along both sides, almost to the bone, to allow the seasonings to penetrate.

In a bowl, combine the rice wine and light soy sauce, then pour over the fish, rubbing into the cuts. Set aside to marinate.

In a separate bowl, mix together the cornflour and 1 tablespoon water to make a smooth paste, then stir in the dark soy sauce, rice wine and sugar. Set aside.

Heat the oil in a wok or large heavy-based frying pan over medium heat. Drain any excess marinade from the fish. When the oil is hot, deep-fry the fish, in batches, for about 3–4 minutes on each side, or until dark brown. Drain on paper towel briefly, then arrange on a serving platter.

Pour off all but 3 tablespoons of oil from the wok and cook the ginger and garlic over medium heat until golden. Add the chilli bean sauce, cornflour mixture and 250 ml (8½ fl oz/1 cup) water and stir constantly until it comes to the boil, clears and thickens. Add the spring onion and stir to combine, then pour the hot sauce over the fish and serve immediately with white rice.

Hoi Seenjeung Boon Yue Lau

Fish fillets with hoisin sauce

Serves: 3–4

375 g (13 oz) skinless, boneless, firm white fish fillets

2 tablespoons oil

1 garlic clove, bruised

1 tablespoon light soy sauce

½ teaspoon finely grated fresh ginger

1 teaspoon hoisin sauce

2 tablespoons thinly sliced spring onion (scallion) to garnish

Wipe the fish with damp paper towel. Cut the fish into serving portions (see page 11).

Heat the oil in a wok or large heavy-based frying pan over medium heat. Add the garlic and cook until golden, then remove the garlic with a slotted spoon and discard. Cook the fish in the flavoured oil, one piece at a time, turning after a few seconds and moving to the side of the wok to make room for the next. When all the fish has been added to the wok, sprinkle with the soy sauce, cover, and simmer for 1 minute. Add the ginger and continue to simmer for a further 1 minute, then remove from the heat and stir in the hoisin sauce to combine. Arrange the fish on a serving platter, spoon over the sauce and garnish with the spring onion. Serve with white rice.

Fun Yue
Fragrant fried fish

Serves: 6

A popular way of preparing fish, this dish can be prepared well in advance, which makes it perfect for entertaining. It should be served at room temperature.

1 kg (2 lb 3 oz) boneless, skinless, firm white fish fillets

3 spring onions (scallions), thinly sliced

1 tablespoon finely grated fresh ginger

1 teaspoon Chinese five-spice

125 ml (4 fl oz/½ cup) light soy sauce

2 tablespoons Chinese rice wine or dry sherry

¼ teaspoon salt

2 teaspoons vinegar

125 ml (4 fl oz/½ cup) Fish stock (page 42)

2½ tablespoons sugar

oil for frying

Wipe the fish with damp paper towel. Cut the fish into serving portions (see page 11).

Take 1 teaspoon each of the spring onion and ginger and put into a deep plate for marinating the fish. Mix in the five-spice, soy sauce, rice wine and salt, stirring to combine. Add the fish and toss gently to coat, then cover and refrigerate for at least 3 hours. Just before starting to cook drain the fish well, pressing out any excess moisture and reserving the marinade. To the marinade, add the vinegar, stock and 2 teaspoons of the sugar.

Put 250 ml (8½ fl oz/1 cup) water and the remaining sugar into a saucepan and stir over low heat until the sugar has dissolved. Simmer over low heat.

Heat the oil in a wok or large heavy-based frying pan over medium heat. When the oil is hot, deep-fry the fish, in batches, for about 1 minute, or until golden. Drain briefly on paper towel, then place into the pan with the simmering syrup and cook for about 1 minute. Remove the fish to a plate; discard the syrup.

Pour off all but 2 tablespoons of oil from the wok, add the reserved onion and ginger and stir-fry over medium heat for 1 minute. Add the fish pieces and toss gently. Add the reserved marinade mixture, bring to the boil, then remove from the heat. Arrange the fish on a serving plate, pour over the sauce and allow to cool to room temperature before serving.

Gwoo Lo Yue Lau
Crisp–skin fish with sweet sour sauce

Serves: 3–4

750 g (1 lb 11 oz) whole snapper or other firm white fish

1 teaspoon salt

½ teaspoon Chinese five-spice

oil for frying

1 egg, lightly beaten

30 g (1 oz/¼ cup) cornflour (cornstarch)

Sweet sour sauce

1 carrot, thinly sliced

3 tablespoons frozen peas

1 tablespoon light soy sauce

1 tablespoon Chinese rice wine or dry sherry

60 ml (2 fl oz/¼ cup) tomato sauce (ketchup)

2 tablespoons vinegar

2 tablespoons sugar

1 tablespoon cornflour (cornstarch)

2 tablespoons peanut oil

1 garlic clove, crushed

1 teaspoon finely grated fresh ginger

1 small onion, chopped

2 tablespoons preserved melon shreds (optional)

Clean and scale the fish, leaving the head on. Wipe inside the fish cavity with damp paper towel that has first been dipped in coarse salt. Trim any long spines or fins neatly. With a sharp knife score vertical cuts along both sides, almost to the bone. In a bowl, combine the salt and five-spice and rub over the fish, inside and out, rubbing into the cuts.

To make the sweet sour sauce, blanch the carrot and peas in a saucepan of salted boiling water, then drain well. In a bowl, combine the soy sauce, rice wine, tomato sauce, vinegar, sugar and 190 ml (6½ fl oz/¾ cup) water and stir until the sugar has dissolved. In a separate bowl, combine the cornflour and 60 ml (2 fl oz/¼ cup) water and stir into the soy mixture.

Heat the peanut oil in a wok or large heavy-based frying pan over medium heat. Add the garlic, ginger, carrot, peas and onion and stir-fry for 2 minutes. Add the sauce mixture, bring to the boil, then add the cornflour mixture and stir until thickened. Remove from the heat and stir in the melon shreds, if using. Set aside and keep warm.

To cook the fish, heat the oil in a wok or large heavy-based frying pan over medium heat. Dip the fish first into the egg and then into the cornflour to coat, shaking off any excess. Gently lower the fish into the hot oil and deep-fry for about 4 minutes on each side, spooning the hot oil over while it cooks. Drain on paper towel and serve immediately with the sweet sour sauce in a bowl on the side.

Ching Chow Ho Yau Har Yan

Stir-fried prawns with oyster sauce

Serves: 3–4

2 tablespoons oil

1 garlic clove, crushed

½ teaspoon finely grated fresh ginger

250 g (9 oz) raw prawns (shrimp), peeled
and deveined

1 tablespoon oyster sauce

2 tablespoons Chinese rice wine or dry
sherry

125 ml (4 fl oz/½ cup) Fish stock (page 42)
or water

2 teaspoons cornflour (cornstarch)

Heat the oil in a wok or large heavy-based frying pan over low heat. Add the garlic and ginger and cook until golden. Add the prawns and stir-fry until they turn pink. Add the oyster sauce, rice wine and stock and bring to the boil. Cover and simmer for 2 minutes. In a small bowl, combine the cornflour and 1 tablespoon cold water to make a smooth paste then stir into the sauce until the liquid thickens and becomes clear. Serve at once with white rice.

Note

You can add vegetables to this dish if you like: stir-fry about 300 g (10½ oz/3 cups) chopped mixed vegetables after cooking the ginger and garlic. Remove them from the wok before adding the prawns and return to the wok to re-heat after the sauce has been made.

Seafood

Sai Lan Far Chow Har Kau
Coral and jade prawns

Serves: 4

12–16 raw large prawns (shrimp), peeled and deveined, tails left intact

300 g (10½ oz) broccoli, broken into small florets with stems attached

1 tablespoon peanut oil

½ teaspoon finely grated fresh ginger

¼ teaspoon salt

1 tablespoon Chinese rice wine or dry sherry

1½ teaspoons cornflour (cornstarch)

1 tablespoon pickled ginger (beni shoga)

Using the point of a sharp knife, make a small slit through the prawn from its underside to the deveined upperside. Pass the end of one broccoli stem through the slit in the underside of the prawn so that the floret rests within the curve of the prawn.

Heat the peanut oil in a wok or large heavy-based frying pan over high heat. Add the ginger and prawns threaded with broccoli and stir-fry for 2 minutes. Add the salt, rice wine and 80 ml (2½ fl oz/⅓ cup) water to the wok, reduce the heat to low, cover, and simmer for 3 minutes.

Push the prawns to one side of the wok. In a small bowl, combine the cornflour and 1 tablespoon cold water to make a smooth paste, then add to the wok and continue stirring until the sauce thickens. Serve immediately, garnished with pickled ginger and accompanied by white rice.

Gai Choy Chow Har Kau
Stir-fried prawns with mustard cabbage

Serves: 3–4

2 tablespoons peanut oil

1 garlic clove, crushed

½ teaspoon finely grated fresh ginger

250 g (9 oz) raw large prawns (shrimp),
peeled and deveined

1 head mustard cabbage (gai choy),
chopped

1 tablespoon light soy sauce

1 tablespoon Chinese rice wine or dry
sherry

¼ teaspoon Chinese five-spice

½ teaspoon salt

1½ teaspoons cornflour (cornstarch)

Heat the oil in a wok or large heavy-based frying pan over high heat. Add the garlic, ginger, prawns and mustard cabbage and stir-fry for 2 minutes, stirring constantly. Combine 1 tablespoon water with the soy sauce, then mix in the rice wine, five-spice and salt. Add to the wok, stir through to coat the prawns and cabbage, then cover and simmer for 5 minutes.

In a small bowl, combine the cornflour and 1 tablespoon cold water and stir to make a smooth paste. Add to the wok and stir until the sauce boils and thickens, about 1 minute. Serve immediately with rice or noodles.

Note

If buying frozen prawns that are already peeled 125 g (4½ oz) will be sufficient for this dish.

Sze Chuen Chow Har Kau
Sichuan prawns with dried chillies

Serves: 6

I have made this recipe using equal quantities of prawns (shrimp) and cooked shelled crab (cracked into large pieces, not flaked crabmeat), and it is delicious. If you do it this way, add the crab to the marinade with the prawns and cook for the same length of time.

500 g (1 lb 2 oz) raw prawns (shrimp), peeled and deveined

1 teaspoon salt

2 teaspoons cornflour (cornstarch)

½ egg white, lightly beaten

Seasonings and sauce

1 teaspoon cornflour (cornstarch)

1 tablespoon light soy sauce

2 teaspoons Chinese rice wine or dry sherry

1½ teaspoons honey or sugar

1 teaspoon white vinegar

½ teaspoon salt

¼ teaspoon freshly ground black pepper

60 ml (2 fl oz/¼ cup) oil

8–10 large dried red chillies, deseeded

2 spring onions (scallions), thinly sliced

1 teaspoon grated or chopped fresh ginger

2 garlic cloves, crushed

Put the prawns into a bowl with 250 ml (8½ fl oz/1 cup) cold water and ½ teaspoon of the salt. Stir and leave for 2 minutes, then rinse and drain well.

In a bowl, combine the cornflour and 1 tablespoon cold water and stir to make a smooth paste. Add the egg white and the remaining salt and stir well, then add the prawns and toss to coat. Leave to marinate for 30 minutes.

To make the sauce, combine the cornflour and 2 tablespoons cold water in a small bowl to make a smooth paste, then stir in the soy sauce, rice wine, honey, vinegar, salt and pepper. Set aside.

Heat the oil in a wok or large heavy-based frying pan over medium heat. Add the chillies and stir-fry for a few seconds, or until almost black. Remove with a slotted spoon and drain on paper towel.

Drain any excess marinade from the prawns, add the prawns to the wok and stir-fry for 20–30 seconds, or until they turn pink. Add the spring onion, ginger and garlic and stir-fry briefly. Add the cornflour mixture and stir constantly until the sauce boils and thickens. Turn off the heat, return the chillies to the wok, stir to mix and serve immediately with white rice.

Note

For a less hot result, discard the oil in which the chillies are fried and heat fresh oil before cooking the remaining ingredients.

Seafood

Ho Lan Dau Chow Dai Tze
Scallops with snow peas

Serves: 2–3

This delicate dish must not be overcooked, so have seasonings measured and cornflour (cornstarch) mixed with water in readiness for adding and serve immediately.

2 tablespoons peanut oil

2 leeks, white part only, thinly sliced

½ teaspoon finely grated fresh ginger

250 g (9 oz) scallops, cleaned

125 g (4½ oz) snow peas (mangetout), trimmed

2 teaspoons cornflour (cornstarch)

1 teaspoon light soy sauce

½ teaspoon salt

Heat the oil in a wok or large heavy-based frying pan over medium heat. Add the leek and ginger and cook for 1 minute. Add the scallops and stir-fry over high heat for 1 minute, then add the snow peas and stir-fry for a further 1 minute. Push the scallops and vegetables to one side of the pan.

In a bowl, combine the cornflour and 60 ml (2 fl oz/¼ cup) cold water to make a smooth paste. Add to the wok with the soy sauce and stir until the sauce thickens, about 1 minute. Stir in the scallops and vegetables to coat, sprinkle with the salt and serve immediately.

See Jiu Chow Loong Har
Quick-fried lobster in hot bean sauce

Serves: 6

....

500 g (1 lb 2 oz) raw lobster tails

60 ml (2 fl oz/¼ cup) oil

1 small green or red capsicum (bell pepper),
deseeded and chopped

2 garlic cloves, crushed

½ teaspoon finely grated fresh ginger

1–2 tablespoons Chinese chilli bean sauce

125 ml (4 fl oz/½ cup) Chicken stock
(page 42) or water

2 tablespoons Chinese rice wine or dry
sherry

1 egg, lightly beaten

2 teaspoons cornflour (cornstarch)

a few drops of sesame oil (optional)

sliced spring onion (scallion) to garnish

Chop the lobster tails into sections and remove the shells.

Heat the oil in a wok or large heavy-based frying pan over high heat. Add the lobster and stir-fry for 1 minute or until just cooked. Remove to a plate. Add the capsicum and stir-fry for 1 minute, or until softened slightly, then remove to a plate.

Reduce the heat, add the garlic and ginger to the oil in the wok and stir-fry briefly, then add the chilli bean sauce and stir-fry for a few seconds. Add the salt, stock and rice wine and bring to the boil. Dribble the egg into the simmering sauce, stirring constantly so that the egg sets into fine shreds.

In a small bowl, combine the cornflour and 1 tablespoon cold water and stir to make a smooth paste. Add to the simmering sauce and stir constantly until it thickens. Add the sesame oil, return the lobster and capsicum to the wok and stir to combine and heat through. Garnish with spring onion and serve with white rice.

Chow Loong Har Kau
Stir-fried lobster with red sauce

Serves: 2–3

250 g (9 oz) raw lobster tails

½ egg white

2 teaspoons Chinese rice wine or dry sherry

½ teaspoon salt

2 teaspoons cornflour (cornstarch)

60 ml (2 fl oz/¼ cup) oil

Sauce

1 small garlic clove, crushed

½ teaspoon finely grated fresh ginger

60 ml (2 fl oz/¼ cup) tomato sauce
  (ketchup)

1 teaspoon chilli sauce

1 tablespoon Chinese vinegar or
  2 teaspoons cider vinegar

2 teaspoons sugar

2 teaspoons cornflour (cornstarch)

80 g (2¾ oz/½ cup) cooked peas (optional)

Chop the lobster tails into sections and remove the shells. Chop the lobster meat into bite-sized chunks. In a bowl, combine the egg white, rice wine, salt and cornflour. Add the lobster and leave to marinate for 20 minutes.

Heat the oil in a wok or large heavy-based frying pan over medium heat. Add the lobster and cook for 2–3 minutes, turning to cook all sides. Remove to a plate.

To make the sauce, pour off all but 1 tablespoon of the oil in the wok. Cook the garlic and ginger over low heat until golden. Add the tomato sauce, chilli sauce, vinegar, sugar and 60 ml (2 fl oz/¼ cup) water and stir until the sugar has dissolved. Bring to the boil.

In a small bowl, combine the cornflour and 1 tablespoon cold water and stir to make a smooth paste. Add to the wok and continue stirring until the sauce thickens. Return the lobster to the wok, add the cooked peas and stir to combine and heat through. Serve immediately with rice.

See Jup Gook Hai
Fried crab in black bean sauce

Serves: 4

This is perhaps the most popular shellfish preparation in Chinese restaurants in Australia. To be enjoyed to the fullest the crab should be picked up in the fingers and eaten.

1.5 kg (3 lb 5 oz) whole fresh crab

1 tablespoon tinned salted black beans, rinsed and drained

1 large garlic clove, crushed, plus 1 extra, halved

1 tablespoon light soy sauce

1 teaspoon sugar

80 ml (2½ fl oz/⅓ cup) peanut oil

2 slices fresh ginger

2 teaspoons cornflour (cornstarch)

3 spring onions (scallions), thinly sliced

1 egg, lightly beaten

Remove the large shell from the crab and discard the fibrous tissue under the shell. Divide the crab into four portions, breaking the body in half and separating the claws, leaving the legs attached. Crack the claws so the sauce can penetrate.

Mash the black beans in a bowl, then add the crushed garlic, soy sauce and sugar and stir well to combine.

Heat the oil in a wok or large heavy-based frying pan over high heat. Add the halved garlic and the ginger and cook until they start to brown, then remove with a slotted spoon and discard. Cook the crab in the flavoured oil, turning constantly for 4–5 minutes or until shells are bright red. Remove to a plate. Add the black bean paste and stir-fry for 1 minute, then add 170 ml (5½ fl oz/⅔ cup) hot water, return the crab to the wok, stir well, cover, and simmer for 3 minutes.

In a bowl, combine the cornflour and 1 tablespoon cold water to make a smooth paste, then add to the wok and continue stirring until the sauce boils and thickens. Add the spring onion and egg and stir until the egg sets. Serve immediately with white rice.

Ho Yau Chang Dau Dew Pin

Squid with green peas in oyster sauce

Serves: 6

Squid is one of the most subtle of seafoods and is best served with a light-flavoured vegetable. This dish combines it with tender young peas and a sauce that tastes of the sea.

500 g (1 lb 2 oz) small squid

2 tablespoons peanut oil

½ teaspoon finely grated fresh ginger

235 g (8½ oz/1½ cups) frozen peas

125 ml (4 fl oz/½ cup) Fish or Chicken stock (page 42)

1 teaspoon light soy sauce

1 tablespoon oyster sauce

2 teaspoons cornflour (cornstarch)

Braised lettuce (page 129) to serve

Clean each squid, removing the ink sac and discarding the head. Separate the tentacles from the body. Discard the tentacles. Rinse under cold running water to remove the skin. Drain well and cut the body lengthways into pieces. Use a sharp knife to score the pieces in a criss-cross pattern.

Heat 1 tablespoon of the oil in a wok or large heavy-based frying pan over high heat. Add the ginger and squid and stir-fry for 2–3 minutes, or until the squid is opaque. Remove to a plate.

Add the remaining peanut oil to the wok and toss the peas in it for a few seconds, then add the stock, soy sauce and oyster sauce and bring to the boil. In a small bowl, combine the cornflour and 1 tablespoon cold water to make a smooth paste, then add to the wok and stir constantly until the sauce thickens. Return the squid and stir to combine and heat through. Serve immediately on a bed of Braised lettuce (page 129).

Poultry

✳

Chan Pei Fun Gai
Smoked tangerine chicken

Serves: 4–5

The subtle smoky anise and citrus notes of this dish are tantalising. Smoking in a pot is easily done without special equipment – all you need is some foil and a large heavy-based saucepan with a tight-fitting lid.

1 tablespoon light soy sauce

1 teaspoon salt

1 teaspoon sugar

1 tablespoon Chinese rice wine or dry sherry

1.5 kg (3 lb 5 oz) whole chicken

1 piece dried tangerine peel

1 whole star anise

3 tablespoons soft brown sugar

fresh coriander (cilantro) leaves to garnish

In a bowl, combine the soy sauce, salt, sugar and rice wine and rub inside and outside the chicken. Allow to marinate for about 20 minutes, then put in a steamer basket and steam over simmering water for 15 minutes.

Using a mortar and pestle, crush the tangerine peel and star anise as finely as possible and mix with the sugar.

Take a large heavy-based saucepan with a tight-fitting lid, large enough to hold the whole chicken. Line the base of the pan with foil, bringing it a little way up the side of the pan. Sprinkle the spice mixture evenly over the foil, then put a trivet or wire rack in the pan and set the chicken on it. Cover and cook over medium heat until smoke starts escaping from under the lid, then reduce the heat to low and smoke the chicken for 15 minutes or until cooked through.

This chicken dish can be served hot, at room temperature, or cold. Slice the flesh off the bones and arrange on a platter, or chop through the bones into small pieces. Garnish with the coriander.

Chu Hau Jeung Mun Gai
Chicken with barbecued oysters

Serves: 4–5

500 g (1 lb 2 oz) boneless skinless chicken breasts, diced

2 teaspoons cornflour (cornstarch), plus 2 teaspoons extra

1 teaspoon Chinese five-spice

1 teaspoon salt

oil for frying

1 garlic clove, crushed

125 ml (4 fl oz/½ cup) Chicken stock (page 42)

175 g (6 oz) tinned oysters, drained

2 tablespoons Chinese barbecue (char siu) sauce

Toss the chicken in a bowl with the cornflour, five-spice and salt.

Heat 2 tablespoons of the oil in a wok or large heavy-based frying pan over high heat. Add the garlic and cook for a few seconds, then add the chicken and stir-fry for 2–3 minutes, or until it starts to colour. Push the chicken to one side of the wok.

In a small bowl, combine the extra cornflour and 2 tablespoons cold water to make a smooth paste. Add the stock to the wok, then add the cornflour mixture and stir constantly until the sauce boils and thickens. Add the oysters and barbecue sauce and toss to coat everything together until heated through. Serve with the rice.

Ling Moong Gai
Lemon chicken

Serves: 4–6

1.5 kg (3 lb 5 oz) whole chicken

2 tablespoons dark soy sauce

finely grated zest of 1 large lemon

80 ml (2½ fl oz/⅓ cup) lemon juice

1 tablespoon sugar

1 teaspoon sesame oil

2 teaspoons shredded fresh ginger

1 teaspoon cornflour (cornstarch)

2 tablespoons thinly sliced spring onion (scallion) to serve

lemon slices to garnish

Cut the chicken into quarters, dry with paper towel and rub with 1 tablespoon of the soy sauce. Set aside.

In a bowl, combine the lemon zest, lemon juice, remaining soy sauce, sugar, sesame oil and 250 ml (8½ fl oz/1 cup) water, stirring to dissolve the sugar.

Heat the oil in a wok or large heavy-based frying pan over medium heat. Add the chicken, skin side down, and cook until brown, then turn to brown the other side. Add the ginger and continue to cook for 1 minute. Add the lemon juice mixture, bring to the boil, then reduce the heat to low, cover, and simmer for 15 minutes, or until the chicken is tender but not falling off the bone. This can be prepared ahead up to this stage, transferred to a dish and left until required. Do not leave it in the metal wok or the acidity of the lemon juice will react with the metal and make the food taste odd.

At serving time, return the chicken and sauce to the wok and heat through. Remove the chicken to a plate, then cut the flesh into bite-sized pieces.

In a bowl, mix together the cornflour and 1 tablespoon cold water and stir to make a smooth paste. Add to the sauce and stir constantly until the sauce boils and thickens. Spoon the hot sauce over the chicken, garnish with the spring onion and lemon slices and serve with white rice.

Ho Yau Mun Gai
Cold chicken in oyster sauce

Serves: 4

500 g (1 lb 2 oz) boneless skinless chicken
  breasts

3 sprigs celery leaves

1 small onion

2 tablespoons honey

1 tablespoon oyster sauce

1 tablespoon light soy sauce

½ teaspoon salt

⅛ teaspoon Chinese five spice

3 tablespoons thinly sliced spring onion
  (scallion)

3 teaspoons finely grated fresh ginger

2 tablespoons lightly toasted sesame seeds

Put the chicken, celery leaves and onion into a large saucepan with enough cold water to cover. Bring to the boil, then reduce the heat to low, cover, and simmer for 10 minutes. Turn off the heat and allow the chicken to cool in the liquid. Remove the chicken with a slotted spoon once cool and thinly slice the meat. Arrange on a plate.

In a bowl, mix together the honey, oyster sauce, soy sauce, salt and five-spice, then spoon over the chicken. Cover and leave for 30 minutes for the flavours to develop. Before serving, sprinkle over the combined spring onion and ginger, then the sesame seeds.

Variation

To make cold lemon chicken with coriander (cilantro), prepare the chicken as above; cool and slice as described. Instead of preparing the oyster sauce, combine 2 tablespoons Chinese lemon sauce and 1 tablespoon Chinese barbecue (char siu) sauce in a bowl. Spoon over the chicken and leave to marinate for 30 minutes. Arrange on a serving dish and serve garnished with 3 tablespoons finely chopped fresh coriander leaves and stems and 1 teaspoon finely grated fresh ginger.

Hai Yook Par Gai

Fried chicken with crab sauce

Serves: 4–6

1 kg (2 lb 3 oz) whole chicken

1 teaspoon salt

2 teaspoons Chinese five-spice

3 tablespoons cornflour (cornstarch) or chestnut flour

peanut oil for deep-frying

Crab sauce

125 g (4½ oz/¾ cup) crabmeat

2 tablespoons peanut oil

½ teaspoon finely grated fresh ginger

6 spring onions (scallions), thinly sliced

190 ml (6½ fl oz/¾ cup) Chicken stock (page 42)

1 egg white, lightly beaten

2½ teaspoons cornflour (cornstarch)

Joint the chicken (see page 10) and cut into serving pieces. Sprinkle the combined salt and five-spice over the chicken and leave for 30 minutes.

To make the crab sauce, flake the crabmeat, removing any bony tissue. Heat the peanut oil in a small saucepan over low heat. Add the ginger and spring onion and cook for 1 minute until soft. Add the stock, bring to the boil, then add the crabmeat and season with freshly ground black pepper. Dribble the egg into the simmering sauce, stirring constantly so that it sets into fine shreds. Combine the cornflour and 1 tablespoon cold water in a bowl to make a smooth paste, then add to the sauce, stirring until the sauce is clear and thick. Remove from the heat and keep warm.

To prepare the chicken, mix together the cornflour and 2 tablespoons cold water in a bowl to make a smooth paste. Heat the peanut oil in a wok or large heavy-based frying pan over medium heat. Dip the chicken into the cornflour paste, drain off any excess, then lower into the hot oil and deep-fry the chicken, in batches, until golden. Drain on paper towel. Arrange on a serving plate, pour the sauce over the top and serve immediately.

Sze Chuen Jar Gai

Fried sichuan chicken

Serves: 6

500 g (1 lb 2 oz) boneless skinless chicken
  breasts

85 g (3 oz/⅔ cup) cornflour (cornstarch),
  plus 2 teaspoons extra

1 teaspoon salt

½ teaspoon Chinese five-spice, plus
  ¼ teaspoon extra

125 ml (4 fl oz/½ cup) Chicken stock
  (page 42)

2 teaspoons sugar

1 tablespoon light soy sauce

½ teaspoon sesame oil

1 teaspoon vinegar

2 teaspoons Chinese rice wine or dry sherry

¼ teaspoon freshly ground black pepper

125 ml (4 fl oz/½ cup) oil

15 large dried red chillies, deseeded

2 garlic cloves, finely chopped

2 teaspoons finely chopped fresh ginger

4 spring onions (scallions), cut into short
  lengths

Cut the chicken into bite-sized pieces. Mix together the cornflour, salt and five-spice and toss to coat the chicken pieces in the mixture, then dust off any excess cornflour.

In a bowl, mix together the stock, sugar, soy sauce, sesame oil, vinegar, rice wine, the extra five-spice and pepper.
In a separate bowl, combine the extra cornflour with 1 tablespoon cold water and stir to make a smooth paste.

Heat the oil in a wok or large heavy-based frying pan over medium heat. When the oil is hot, deep-fry the chicken, in batches, turning until brown all over. Remove with a slotted spoon and drain on paper towel. Repeat until all the chicken is cooked.

Pour off all but 2 tablespoons of the oil from the wok and cook the chillies, garlic and ginger until the chillies turn dark. Add the spring onion and toss for a few seconds, then add the stock mixture and bring to the boil. Add the cornflour paste and stir constantly until the sauce boils and thickens. Add the chicken and toss to heat through. Serve immediately with rice.

Mut Jup Mun Gai Yik
Honey–soy braised chicken wings

Serves: 5–6

....

1 kg (2 lb 3 oz) chicken wings

2 tablespoons peanut oil

80 ml (2½ fl oz/⅓ cup) dark soy sauce

2 tablespoons honey

2 tablespoons Chinese rice wine or dry
sherry

1 garlic clove, crushed

½ teaspoon finely grated fresh ginger

Cut each chicken wing into three pieces and reserve the wing tips for stock. Heat the peanut oil in a wok or large heavy-based frying pan over high heat. Add the chicken and stir-fry for 3–4 minutes, or until browned. Add the soy sauce, honey, rice wine, garlic and ginger and stir to coat. Reduce the heat to low, cover, and simmer for about 30 minutes, or until the chicken wings are tender. Towards the end of cooking, stir frequently and make sure the sweet glaze does not burn. Serve warm or at room temperature.

Ze Gheung Mun Gai
Braised ginger chicken with lily buds

Serves: 4–6

Try to get hold of sichuan pepper – not really a pepper, but the berries of the prickly ash tree, known in Japan as sansho. If they are whole, remove the black seeds as they are very gritty. The effect of this spice is a tongue-tingling, mildly numbing sensation. If you can't find any, substitute with black peppercorns.

1 kg (2 lb 3 oz) whole chicken

20–30 dried lily buds (golden needles)

10 sichuan peppercorns, husks only (glossary)

2 tablespoons peanut oil

1 tablespoon thinly sliced fresh ginger

1 garlic clove, crushed with a pinch of salt

80 ml (2½ fl oz/⅓ cup) Chinese rice wine or dry sherry

1 tablespoon honey

60 ml (2 fl oz/¼ cup) light soy sauce

1 segment star anise

Joint the chicken (see page 10) and cut into serving pieces.

Soak the lily buds in hot water for 20 minutes, then drain well. Pinch off the tough stem end and cut the buds into two or three pieces each.

Heat the sichuan pepper in a dry frying pan over low heat, then crush using a mortar and pestle.

Heat the peanut oil in a wok or large heavy-based frying pan over low heat. Add the ginger and garlic and cook until pale golden. Add the chicken, increase the heat to medium and stir-fry until the chicken changes colour. Add the lily buds, sichuan pepper, rice wine, honey, soy sauce and star anise. Cover and simmer over low heat for 25 minutes, adding a little hot water towards the end of cooking to prevent the sauce sticking to the pan.

Tze Bao Gai
Chicken fried in paper

Makes: about 24

Look for the Chinese rice paper for this one – translucent, baking paper-like squares of pressed cooked rice that melt in the mouth. You won't be able to use Vietnamese rice paper (banh trang), as it is too brittle when dry and once wet, it won't get crisp if deep-fried.

500 g (1 lb 2 oz) boneless skinless chicken breasts, thinly sliced

1 teaspoon light soy sauce

2 teaspoons oyster sauce

1 teaspoon sesame oil

1 tablespoon Chinese rice wine or dry sherry

1 teaspoon sugar

¼ teaspoon salt

1 tablespoon shredded fresh ginger

4 spring onions (scallions), thinly sliced

24 snow peas (mangetout) or sugar snap peas (optional)

twenty-four 13 cm (5 in) squares rice paper or baking paper

oil for deep-frying

Put the chicken into a bowl with the soy sauce, oyster sauce, sesame oil, rice wine, sugar and salt and toss to coat. Leave for 30–60 minutes before cooking.

Place a little of the filling just off centre on each square of rice paper – each piece of paper should contain a slice or two of chicken, one or two shreds of ginger, a slice or two of spring onion and, if liked, a snow pea. When the snow peas and sugar snap peas are out of season simply omit them – do not use another vegetable in their place.

Fold in the sides then roll up the parcel, tucking in the flap of the 'envelope' securely. Repeat with the remaining filling and rice paper squares.

Heat the oil in a wok or large heavy-based frying pan over medium heat. When the oil is hot, deep-fry the parcels, in batches, for about 1–2 minutes, or until golden brown. Drain on paper towel and serve immediately.

Note

When rice paper is used, the chicken can be eaten, envelope and all. If using baking paper, open at the table, lift the contents out and serve with your favourite sauce.

Buck Ging Ngap
Peking duck

Serves: 6

One duck yields three separate dishes, for after the crisp skin is eaten with mandarin pancakes (this is the most important course and what is meant by 'Peking duck') the flesh is served separately and the bones used to make a rich soup. But of course the soup needs long simmering and cannot be served at the same meal. Having had a demonstration in Hong Kong of how to make and how to carve this famous dish I decided that, delicious though it is, it is too time-consuming to prepare often. But for those who, like me, are willing to try anything at least once, here's the best method. Try to get a duck complete with head – not an easy task in these days of politely packaged frozen poultry devoid of all extremities; if you have access to a Chinese delicatessen, however, they may be purchased there. The vodka is not traditional, but it works!

2.5 kg (5½ lb) duck

2 teaspoons salt

80 ml (2½ fl oz/⅓ cup) vodka

1 tablespoon honey

Mandarin pancakes (page 37) to serve

spring onion (scallion) to serve

hoisin sauce to serve

1 cucumber, peeled, seeds removed and thinly sliced lengthways

Wash the duck, drain well and dry thoroughly with paper towel, inside and out. Pick off any pin feathers or quills that remain. Rub the salt inside the body cavity and put the duck on a large plate. Spoon the vodka over and rub all over the duck. Leave for 4 hours, turning the bird from time to time so all the skin is in contact with the vodka.

In a bowl, stir the honey in 750 ml (25½ fl oz/3 cups) hot water until dissolved. Rub this mixture into the skin of the duck to coat. Truss the bird and tie a string around its neck, then hang the duck in front of an electric fan or, if the weather is cool enough, in a breezy place. Leave it to dry for at least 4 hours. (The Chinese chef inflated the skin of the bird, before hanging it, by blowing through a tiny hole in the skin of the duck's neck just above where he would tie the string. He did it as effortlessly as if blowing up a child's balloon, but it isn't as easy as it looked.) If the duck has no head, tie a piece of kitchen string around the top of the neck.

Preheat the oven to 190°C (375°F). Put the duck on a rack in a roasting tin with hot water in it. The duck must be well above the water. Cook for 30 minutes, then reduce the oven temperature to 150°C (300°F) and continue roasting for 1 hour. Increase the heat to 190°C again and continue roasting until the skin is crisp and brown all over and the duck is tender. Remove from the oven and serve with accompaniments.

The duck is carved at the table, only the skin being cut away into thin pieces. These are put on a flat plate and presented ungarnished to guests. Each guest places a piece of skin on a pancake, dips a spring onion brush into hoisin sauce and brushes it over the pancake and duck, then wraps the spring onion and a few cucumber slivers into the pancake and eats it. The duck meat can also be carved and served on a separate plate for eating with the pancakes. Alternatively, the flesh of the duck is cut away from the bones in slivers, quickly stir-fried with spring onion, capsicum (bell pepper) or fresh bean sprouts, and served as a separate course.

Shiu Ng Heung Gai
Oven-roasted spiced chicken

Serves: 6-8

This method of preparation is particularly suitable for chicken drumsticks, thighs or wings. If it is not possible to buy selected joints, a whole chicken can be used. See the variation at end of the recipe.

80 ml (2½ fl oz/⅓ cup) light soy sauce

60 ml (2 fl oz/¼ cup) peanut oil

1 tablespoon Chinese rice wine or dry sherry

1 garlic clove crushed with ½ teaspoon salt

½ teaspoon finely grated fresh ginger

2 teaspoons Chinese five-spice

1.5 kg (3 lb 5 oz) chicken thighs, wings or drumsticks

In a large shallow dish mix together the soy sauce, peanut oil, rice wine, garlic, ginger and five-spice. Add the chicken and toss to coat, then cover and leave to marinate for at least 1 hour.

Preheat the oven to 180°C (350°F). Drain the chicken, reserving the marinade, and arrange the chicken in an even layer, skin side up, in a deep roasting tin. Spoon over about 2 tablespoons of the marinade to cover and roast in the oven for 45–60 minutes, or until the chicken is brown and crisp, basting every 20 minutes with the marinade. Serve hot or cold.

Variation

If you prefer to roast a whole chicken, choose one that is about 1.75 kg (3 lb 14 oz). Prepare the marinade as directed and rub this over the chicken to coat, spooning some into the cavity as well. Marinate for 1 hour, then place in the roasting tin, breast side down, and cook for 1¾ hours, turning the chicken halfway through cooking so it browns all over and basting regularly. To serve, carve the chicken as for Red-cooked chicken (page 98).

Pei Par Ngap
Barbecue-style roast duck

Serves: 4

1.75 kg (3 lb 14 oz) whole duck

1 garlic clove, crushed

1 teaspoon finely grated fresh ginger

1 teaspoon hoisin sauce

1 teaspoon sesame paste (glossary)

1 tablespoon honey

1 tablespoon light soy sauce

1 teaspoon salt

½ teaspoon freshly ground black pepper

Wash the duck well, then dry inside and out with paper towel. Preheat the oven to 180°C (350°F).

Combine all the remaining ingredients in a small saucepan and stir over low heat until the honey melts and the mixture is smooth. Simmer for 2 minutes, adding a spoonful of water if it seems too thick. Remove from the heat and allow to cool slightly, then rub the marinade all over the duck, inside and out. Reserve any remaining marinade to serve as a sauce. Leave to marinate for up to 1 hour.

Put the duck into an oven bag or wrap it in foil. If using an oven bag follow the manufacturer's instructions and pierce a few holes in the bag for steam to escape. Sit the duck, breast side down, in a deep roasting tin and cook for 45 minutes. Turn the duck and cook for a further 45–60 minutes, or until browned all over. Carve the duck into pieces and serve hot with the reserved marinade, Mandarin pancakes (page 37), spring onion (scallion) and plum or hoisin sauce.

Heung So Ngap
Steamed and deep-fried duck

Serves 4

....

2 kg (4 lb 6 oz) duck

1½ teaspoons salt

¼ teaspoon ground sichuan peppercorns
(glossary)

1 tablespoon light soy sauce

2 teaspoons Chinese rice wine or dry sherry

1 teaspoon Chinese five-spice

2–3 teaspoons cornflour (cornstarch)

oil for deep-frying

spring onion (scallion), or fresh coriander
(cilantro) leaves to garnish

Wash the duck well, then dry inside and out with
paper towel.

In a bowl, combine the salt, sichuan pepper, soy sauce, rice
wine and five-spice. Rub all over the duck, inside and out.
Leave to marinate for at least 1 hour.

Place the duck on a steamer rack and steam over a pan of
simmering water for 1¼–1½ hours, or until tender. Remove
the duck from the steamer rack and sprinkle over the
cornflour to coat.

Heat the oil in a wok or large heavy-based frying pan over
medium heat. When the oil is hot, deep-fry the duck,
spooning the oil over if it is not immersed so that it cooks
evenly. Turn the duck when the underside is done and fry
the other side in the same manner until the skin is crisp.
Drain on paper towel and chop the duck into bite-sized
pieces. Garnish with the spring onion and serve hot with
plain white rice.

Baw Law Gai
Chicken with pineapple

Serves: 4–6

This dish provides interesting flavour contrasts between the sweet tang of pineapple and the stinging bite of sichuan pepper.

½ teaspoon ground sichuan peppercorns, husks only (glossary), or black pepper

1 tablespoon cornflour (cornstarch)

½ teaspoon salt

250 g (9 oz) boneless skinless chicken breasts, thinly sliced

1 tablespoon light soy sauce

2 teaspoons sesame oil

1 small garlic clove, crushed

1 tablespoon peanut oil

½ small ripe pineapple, chopped, or 425 g (15 oz/2⅔ cups) tinned unsweetened pineapple, drained

6 spring onions (scallions), thinly sliced

fresh coriander (coriander) leaves to garnish

Sauce

125 ml (4 fl oz/½ cup) pineapple juice

2 teaspoons cornflour (cornstarch)

1 tablespoon light soy sauce

Use a mortar and pestle to grind the sichuan pepper, then pass through a fine sieve, discarding the seeds. In a bowl, combine the cornflour, salt and sichuan pepper, then add the chicken and mix well to coat. Add the soy sauce, sesame oil and garlic and mix well.

To make the sauce, combine the pineapple juice and cornflour in a bowl and stir until smooth. Stir in the soy sauce. Set aside.

Heat the peanut oil in a wok or large heavy-based frying pan over medium heat. Add the chicken and stir-fry until it changes colour. Add the pineapple, reduce the heat, cover and simmer for 3 minutes. Add the sauce and stir until thickened, then add the spring onion and toss to combine. Garnish with the coriander leaves and serve with rice or noodles.

See Yo Gai
Red-cooked chicken

Serves: 4–5

'Red cooking' is the term applied to cooking in dark soy sauce. The liquid that remains after cooking is called a 'master sauce', and can be frozen or refrigerated for future use. The sauce should then be used to cook meat or poultry at least once a week to keep it 'alive'. Cook chicken drumsticks this way for taking on picnics or serving at buffet parties.

1.75 kg (3 lb 14 oz) whole chicken

375 ml (12½ fl oz/1½ cups) dark soy sauce

60 ml (2 fl oz/¼ cup) Chinese rice wine or dry sherry

1 tablespoon thinly sliced fresh ginger

1 garlic clove

1 whole star anise

1½ tablespoons sugar

2 teaspoons sesame oil

Choose a saucepan into which the chicken will fit snugly – it needs to be covered in as much of the soy liquid as possible. Put the chicken into the pan, breast side down, then add all the remaining ingredients, except the sesame oil. Add 375 ml (12½ fl oz/1½ cups) water and bring to the boil, then reduce the heat to low, cover, and simmer for 5 minutes. Turn the chicken over, cover, and simmer for a further 20 minutes, basting the breast every 5 minutes. Remove from the heat and leave covered in the saucepan until cool.

Lift the chicken out of the sauce, place on a serving platter and brush with sesame oil – this gives the chicken a glistening appearance as well as extra flavour. Traditionally, red-cooked chicken is put on a chopping board and cut in half lengthways with a sharp cleaver. Each half is chopped into 3.5 cm (1½ in) strips and reassembled in its original shape. Serve at room temperature with some of the cooking liquid as a dipping sauce.

Lut Tze-Mun Ngap
Braised duck with chestnuts

Serves: 6

....

125 g (4½ oz) dried chestnuts

2 kg (4 lb 6 oz) whole duck

2 garlic cloves, crushed

1 teaspoon finely grated fresh ginger

1 tablespoon light soy sauce

1 tablespoon Chinese rice wine or dry sherry

125 ml (4 fl oz/½ cup) peanut oil

3 tablespoons red tofu (dow foo) (glossary)

2 teaspoons sugar

4 spring onions (scallions), cut into short lengths

Note

Chinese yam or even the humble potato can be used to replace the dried chestnuts. In either case, peel and cut into cubes, then add to the simmering sauce 30 minutes before the duck is cooked.

Put the dried chestnuts in a bowl, pour over enough boiling water to cover and soak for 30 minutes. Drain well, pour over fresh boiling water and soak again for a further 30 minutes. Drain well.

Wash the duck, drain well and dry thoroughly with paper towel, inside and out. Pick off any pin feathers or quills that remain.

In a bowl, combine the garlic, ginger, soy sauce and rice wine and rub all over the duck, inside and out. Heat the peanut oil in a wok or large heavy-based frying pan and brown the duck all over, turning often. Remove to a plate and pour off the oil, leaving only 1 tablespoon. Return the duck to the wok, add the tofu mashed with the sugar. Pour in enough hot water to come halfway up the duck, then add the chestnuts and bring to the boil. Reduce the heat to low, cover, and simmer for about 1¼–1½ hours, turning during cooking, or until the duck is tender – you may need to add more boiling water if the sauce reduces too much – it should coat the back of a spoon. Lift the duck onto a wooden chopping board and cut into pieces with a sharp cleaver, Chinese-style (see page 10). Arrange the duck on a serving dish, spoon the chestnuts and sauce over and garnish with the spring onion.

Sze Chuen Shiu Ngap
Sichuan roast duck

Serves: 4–5

3 kg (6 lb 10 oz) whole duck

3 teaspoons salt

3 teaspoons sichuan peppercorns, husks only (glossary), or whole black peppercorns

1 whole fresh coriander (cilantro) plant, including leaves and stem

1½ teaspoons finely grated fresh ginger

4 spring onions (scallions), chopped

½ teaspoon Chinese five-spice

1 tablespoon honey

1 tablespoon Chinese rice wine or dry sherry

2 teaspoons sesame oil

1 tablespoon light soy sauce

½ teaspoon red food colouring (optional)

Wash the duck, drain well and dry thoroughly with paper towel, inside and out. Pick off any pin feathers or quills that remain. Rub all over with the salt.

Roast the pepper in a dry frying pan for a few minutes, then crush coarsely using a mortar and pestle. If using sichuan pepper, strain through a sieve to remove the seeds. Chop the coriander leaves and stem, reserving the well-washed root.

In a bowl, combine the coriander leaves and stem, ginger, spring onion, five-spice, honey, rice wine, sesame oil, soy sauce and red food colouring, if using. Rub the mixture inside and outside the duck to coat. Put the coriander root inside the cavity. Cover with plastic wrap or foil and refrigerate for at least 4 hours, or overnight.

Preheat the oven to 180°C (350°F). Half-fill a roasting tin with hot water and put a rack in the tin; the water should not reach the rack. Put the duck on the rack, breast side up, and cook for 30 minutes. Cover with foil and continue cooking for another 30 minutes. Reduce the oven temperature to 150°C (300°F), turn the duck over, put foil over it and roast for a further 30 minutes. Turn the duck breast side up once more and continue cooking for 30 minutes, then remove the foil and allow the duck to brown for 15–20 minutes. Carve the duck and serve with Mandarin pancakes (page 37), plum sauce and spring onions cut into short lengths.

Seen Goo Gai Lau To Yan

Chicken and walnuts with straw mushrooms

Serves: 4

3 teaspoons cornflour (cornstarch), plus
  1 teaspoon extra

1 teaspoon salt

½ teaspoon Chinese five-spice

500 g (1 lb 2 oz) boneless skinless chicken
  breasts, diced

oil for deep-frying

125 g (4½ oz/1 cup) walnuts or blanched
  almonds

6 spring onions (scallions), cut into short
  lengths

430 g (15 oz) tinned straw mushrooms,
  drained and halved

1 tinned bamboo shoot, diced

125 ml (4 fl oz/½ cup) Chicken stock
  (page 42)

1 teaspoon light soy sauce

In a bowl, combine the cornflour, salt and five-spice. Add the chicken and toss well to coat.

Heat the oil in a wok or large heavy-based frying pan over medium heat. When the oil is hot, deep-fry the walnuts briefly until golden. Remove with a slotted spoon and drain on paper towel. Deep-fry the chicken, in batches, for 1 minute, or until it changes colour. Remove with a slotted spoon and drain on paper towel.

Pour off all but 2 tablespoons of the oil from the wok. Add the spring onion, straw mushroom and bamboo shoot and stir-fry over high heat for 1 minute. Add the stock and stir to combine. In a bowl, combine the extra cornflour and 1 tablespoon cold water and stir to make a smooth paste. Add to the wok with the soy sauce and stir until the sauce boils and thickens. Return the chicken to the wok and heat through. Turn off the heat, stir in the nuts and serve immediately with rice or noodles.

Sai Lan Far Gai Pin Har Kau
Chicken and prawns with broccoli

Serves: 4–6

500 g (1 lb 2 oz) boneless skinless chicken breasts, thinly sliced

375 g (13 oz) raw prawns (shrimp), peeled, deveined and halved lengthways

½ teaspoon Chinese five-spice

½ teaspoon salt

60 g (2 oz/1 cup) broccoli florets

2 tablespoons peanut oil

1 garlic clove, crushed

½ teaspoon finely grated fresh ginger

2 teaspoons light soy sauce

1 tablespoon Chinese rice wine or dry sherry

2 tablespoons Chicken stock (page 42) or water

1 teaspoon arrowroot or cornflour (cornstarch)

In a bowl, combine the chicken, prawns, five-spice and salt and toss well to coat.

Blanch the broccoli florets in a saucepan of boiling water for 3 minutes, then refresh immediately in cold water, drain and set aside.

Heat the peanut oil in a wok or large heavy-based frying pan over high heat. Add the garlic and ginger and stir-fry for 30 seconds, then add the chicken and prawns and stir-fry until the chicken turns white and the prawns turn pink. Add the soy sauce, rice wine and stock and allow to simmer for 2 minutes.

In a bowl, combine the arrowroot with 1 tablespoon cold water and stir to make a smooth paste. Add to the wok and stir until the sauce boils and thickens. Add the broccoli and toss gently to mix and heat through. Serve hot with rice.

Poultry ✾

Meat

*

Jing Ng Far Nam
Steamed five-flowered pork

Serves: 6

Fragrant with spice, this delicious pork dish is so rich that it must be eaten with plenty of white rice. It is a meal best suited to cold weather.

80 ml (2½ fl oz/⅓ cup) dark soy sauce

2 tablespoons Chinese rice wine or dry sherry

½ teaspoon Chinese five-spice (optional)

1 garlic clove, crushed

1 kg (2 lb 3 oz) lean pork belly, skin removed and cut into large cubes

110 g (4 oz/½ cup) short-grain rice

In a bowl, combine the soy sauce, rice wine, five-spice, if using, and garlic. Add the pork and toss to coat, then set aside for at least 1 hour.

Put the uncooked rice in a wok or large heavy-based frying pan over medium–low heat and stir constantly for about 15 minutes, or until the grains are golden. Transfer to a food processor and grind to a fine powder.

Add the pork to the rice powder to coat each piece, then arrange in a heatproof dish. Place the dish over a saucepan of boiling water, cover, and steam the pork for 2 hours, or until it is so tender it falls apart. Serve hot with white rice.

Char Shiu
Barbecued pork

Serves: 4–6

....

3 garlic cloves, crushed with 1 teaspoon salt

½ teaspoon finely grated fresh ginger

1 tablespoon light soy sauce

1 tablespoon honey

1 tablespoon Chinese rice wine or dry sherry

½ teaspoon Chinese five-spice

500 g (1 lb 2 oz) lean pork belly slices, skin removed

Preheat the oven to 220°C (430°F). In a bowl, combine the garlic, ginger, soy sauce, honey, rice wine and five-spice. Add the pork and toss to coat. Leave to marinate for at least 15 minutes.

Half-fill a roasting tin with hot water and put a wire rack in the tin. Place the pork on the rack and cook for 30 minutes. Turn the pork strips over, brush with the remaining marinade and cook for a further 15 minutes, or until well glazed and starting to caramelise. Cut in slices to serve. Serve immediately with plum sauce or hoisin sauce for dipping.

Gwoo Lo Yook
Crisp-fried pork with sweet sour sauce

Serves: 4–6

1 tablespoon light soy sauce

1 tablespoon Chinese rice wine or dry sherry

½ teaspoon salt

¼ teaspoon freshly ground black pepper

¼ teaspoon Chinese five-spice

500 g (1 lb 2 oz) pork fillet (tenderloin), loin or shoulder, trimmed of fat and cut into bite-sized cubes

150 g (5½ oz/1 cup) plain (all-purpose) flour

1 tablespoon peanut oil, plus extra for deep-frying

1 egg white

Sweet sour sauce:

1 tablespoon light soy sauce

1 tablespoon Chinese rice wine or dry sherry (optional)

60 ml (2 fl oz/¼ cup) tomato sauce (ketchup)

2 tablespoons white vinegar

2 tablespoons white sugar

1 tablespoon cornflour (cornstarch)

2 tablespoons peanut oil

1 small onion, cut into large chunks

1 garlic clove, crushed

¼ teaspoon finely grated fresh ginger

80 g (2¾ oz/½ cup) sliced water chestnuts

1 red capsicum (bell pepper), deseeded and diced

3 tablespoons frozen green peas

2 tablespoons preserved melon shreds (optional)

In a bowl, mix together the soy sauce, rice wine, salt, pepper and five-spice. Add the pork, toss to coat, and then cover and refrigerate until needed.

In a separate bowl, combine the flour and 190 ml (6½ fl oz/ ¾ cup) lukewarm water to make a smooth batter. Stir in the peanut oil and set aside for 30 minutes. Beat the egg white until stiff, then fold into the batter.

Heat the oil in a wok or large heavy-based frying pan over medium heat. Dip the pork in the batter to coat. When the oil is hot, deep-fry the pork, in batches, until golden. Drain on paper towel and set aside, reserving the oil in the wok.

To make the sweet sour sauce, combine the soy sauce, rice wine, tomato sauce, vinegar, sugar and 190 ml (6½ fl oz/ ¾ cup) water in a bowl and stir until the sugar has dissolved. In a separate bowl, combine the cornflour and 1 tablespoon cold water and stir to make a smooth paste.

Heat the peanut oil in a saucepan over medium heat. Add the onion, garlic, ginger, water chestnuts, capsicum and peas and stir-fry for 2 minutes. Add the soy sauce mixture, bring to the boil, then add the cornflour paste and stir constantly until the sauce boils and thickens. Remove from the heat and stir in the melon shreds, if using. Keep warm.

Just before serving, re-heat the reserved oil in the wok over medium heat. When the oil is hot, deep-fry the pork again for just a few seconds to make the batter very crisp. Remove with a slotted spoon and drain on paper towel. To serve, arrange on a plate, pour the sweet sour sauce over and serve immediately.

Lut Gee Hoong Shiu Ju Yook
Braised pork with chestnuts

Serves: 4–6

2 garlic cloves, crushed with 1 teaspoon salt

1 tablespoon light soy sauce

1 tablespoon Chinese rice wine or brandy

750 g (1 lb 11 oz) lean pork belly, skin removed and diced

125 g (4½ oz) dried chestnuts

2 tablespoons peanut oil

2 teaspoons cornflour (cornstarch)

2 tablespoons thinly sliced spring onion (scallion) to garnish

In a bowl, combine the garlic, soy sauce and rice wine. Add the pork and leave to marinate for 1 hour.

Put the chestnuts in a separate bowl and pour over enough boiling water to cover. Leave to soak for 30 minutes. Drain, then pour over more fresh boiling water and soak for a further 30 minutes. Drain well.

Heat the peanut oil in a wok or large heavy-based frying pan over high heat. Add the pork and stir-fry for 3 minutes, or until brown. Add the chestnuts and stir well, then add 625 ml (21 fl oz/2½ cups) hot water, cover, and simmer for 35–40 minutes.

In a small bowl, combine the cornflour and 2 tablespoons cold water to make a smooth paste. Push the pork and chestnuts to one side of the wok, then add the cornflour mixture and stir constantly until the sauce boils and thickens – you should have about 1 cup of sauce in the wok, if not, add water to make up this amount. Garnish with the spring onion and serve with rice.

Ju Yook Ma Tai Chow Hahm Suen Choy

Sliced pork and water chestnut roll with sweet and sour vegetables

Serves: 8

500 g (1 lb 2 oz) minced (ground) pork

175 g (6 oz/1 cup) chopped water chestnuts

1 garlic clove, crushed

1 teaspoon salt

1 tablespoon cornflour (cornstarch)

3 tablespoons finely chopped spring onion (scallion)

½ teaspoon Chinese five-spice (optional)

1 egg, beaten

oil for deep-frying

fresh coriander (cilantro) leaves to garnish

Batter

75 g (2¾ oz/½ cup) plain (all-purpose) flour

2 teaspoons oil

Sweet and sour vegetables:

440 g (15½ oz) tinned pineapple pieces, drained and 190 ml (6½ fl oz/¾ cup) syrup reserved

100 g (3½ oz) chow chow preserves, drained, chopped and 2 tablespoons liquid reserved

60 ml (2 fl oz/¼ cup) white vinegar

3 tablespoons sugar

red food colouring (optional)

¾ teaspoon salt

10 spring onions (scallions), cut into short lengths

1 carrot, cut into thin matchsticks

2 tablespoons sliced water chestnuts

1 tablespoon arrowroot

In a bowl, combine the minced pork with the water chestnuts, garlic, salt, cornflour, spring onion, five-spice and egg. Mix thoroughly, then divide the mixture into three even-sized portions and form each portion into a roll, about 17 cm (6¾ in) long. Place on a lightly oiled heatproof plate in a steamer, cover, and steam for 20–25 minutes. Cool completely and chill for a short while, if possible, to firm up.

Meanwhile, make the batter. Put the flour, oil and 190 ml (6½ fl oz/¾ cup) water into a bowl and beat until smooth. Leave to stand for 30 minutes.

To make the sweet and sour vegetables, put the pineapple syrup and chow chow liquid into a saucepan with the vinegar, and sugar and stir well to combine. Bring to the boil and add a pinch of red food colouring, if using – it should be a bright, clear flamingo pink, not deep red. Add the salt, pineapple pieces, spring onion, carrot and water chestnuts, and bring back to the boil. In a small bowl, combine the arrowroot and 1 tablespoon cold water to make a smooth paste, then add to the pan and stir constantly until boiling and thick. Remove from the heat and keep warm.

Cut the rolls into 2 cm (¾ in) slices. Heat the oil in a wok or large heavy-based frying pan over medium heat. Working with a few slices at a time, dip them into the batter, then gently lower into the hot oil and deep-fry, in batches, until golden. Drain on paper towel, then arrange on a serving platter. Pour over the sweet and sour vegetables and garnish with the coriander.

Ngau Yook Ju Yook Yin
Beef and pork balls with rice coating

Serves: 4–6

There are two names for this recipe – one is pearl balls and the other porcupine balls, because the rice grains stick out like the quills of a porcupine.

220 g (8 oz/1 cup) short-grain rice

6 dried shiitake mushrooms

250 g (9 oz) lean minced (ground) beef

250 g (9 oz) minced (ground) pork

3 spring onions (scallions), thinly sliced

½ teaspoon finely grated fresh ginger

1 garlic clove, crushed

2 teaspoons salt

1 egg, lightly beaten

45 g (1½ oz/¼ cup) finely chopped water chestnuts

Put the rice in a bowl with enough cold water to cover and leave to soak for at least 2 hours, then drain well. Spread out on a tray lined with paper towel and leave to dry while preparing the meatballs.

Soak the mushrooms in hot water for 20–30 minutes, then drain well. Cut off and discard the mushroom stems and thinly slice the caps. Put into a large bowl with all the remaining ingredients and use your hands to combine everything together evenly.

Take portions of the mixture at a time and roll into balls with a 2.5 cm (1 in) diameter, rolling them between your palms. Roll each ball separately in the rice, making sure you press just hard enough for the rice to stick and make an even coat all over.

Lightly oil a bamboo steamer basket and arrange the balls in the base, leaving space between each so the rice can swell as it steams. Steam over boiling water for about 30–35 minutes, or until the rice swells and the balls are covered in pearly grains – you may need to add more boiling water during this time. Serve immediately.

Ng Heung Ngau Yook Szee
Shredded five-spice beef

Serves: 4–6

500 g (1 lb 2 oz) tender beef rump (round) or fillet

1 garlic clove, crushed with 1 teaspoon salt

½ teaspoon finely grated fresh ginger

1 tablespoon dark soy sauce

½ teaspoon Chinese five-spice

2 teaspoons cornflour (cornstarch)

2 tablespoons peanut oil

Partially freeze the beef and slice it very thinly, then continue slicing into shreds.

In a bowl, combine the garlic, ginger and soy sauce. Add the shredded beef and toss to coat. Sprinkle over the combined five-spice and cornflour and toss to combine.

Heat the peanut oil in a wok or large heavy-based frying pan over high heat. Add the beef and stir-fry until it changes colour. Add 1 tablespoon water, stir well and bring to the boil; continue boiling until the liquid has thickened. Serve immediately with rice or noodles.

Note

You can add vegetables to this dish if desired. Use 500 g (1 lb 2 oz) vegetables – try a combination of Chinese cabbage (wombok), green beans, broccoli, onion, cauliflower or celery. If using green beans, cauliflower or broccoli, blanch them first in boiling water for 2 minutes and drain before adding to the dish, but other vegetables can be added raw and stir-fried for 2 minutes.

See Jup Ngau Yook
Beef in black bean sauce

Serves: 4–6

500 g (1 lb 2 oz) lean rump (round) or fillet steak

1½ tablespoons tinned salted black beans, rinsed and drained

1 tablespoon dark soy sauce

60 ml (2 fl oz/¼ cup) water or stock

1 teaspoon sugar

1 teaspoon cornflour (cornstarch)

2 tablespoons peanut oil

1 teaspoon sesame oil (optional)

2 garlic cloves, crushed

Trim any fat from the beef, then freeze the beef for 1 hour or just until firm enough to cut into paper-thin slices.

Use a fork to mash the black beans in a bowl, then add the soy sauce, water and sugar. In a separate bowl, combine the cornflour and 2 teaspoons cold water to make a smooth paste. Set aside.

Heat the peanut oil and sesame oil, if using, in a wok or large heavy-based frying pan over high heat. Add the beef and stir-fry until it changes colour. Add the garlic and toss for a few seconds, then add the bean mixture and bring to the boil. Reduce the heat to low, cover, and simmer for about 5 minutes. Add the cornflour paste and stir constantly until the sauce is clear and thick. Serve immediately with white rice.

Lin Ngau Chow Ngau Yook

Beef with lotus root

Serves: 3–4

250 g (9 oz) lean rump (round) or fillet steak

1 tablespoon light soy sauce

½ teaspoon salt

1 garlic clove, crushed

½ teaspoon finely grated fresh ginger

¼ teaspoon Chinese five-spice

2 tablespoons peanut oil

125 ml (4 fl oz/½ cup) Beef stock (page 43) or water

1 tablespoon cornflour (cornstarch)

12 slices frozen lotus root

Trim any fat from the beef, then freeze the beef for 1 hour or just until firm enough to cut into paper-thin slices.

In a bowl, combine the soy sauce, salt, garlic, ginger and five-spice. Add the beef and toss to coat.

Heat the peanut oil in a wok or large heavy-based frying pan over high heat. Add the beef and stir-fry until the colour changes.

In a small bowl, combine the cornflour and 2 tablespoons cold water, stirring to make a smooth paste. Add the stock to the wok, then add the cornflour paste and stir constantly until the sauce boils and thickens. Add the lotus root and stir to combine and heat through. Serve with white rice.

Ho Lan Dau Chow Ngau Yook
Beef with snow peas

Serves: 4–6

500 g (1 lb 2 oz) lean rump (round) or fillet
 steak

2 tablespoons light soy sauce

½ teaspoon salt

6 dried shiitake mushrooms

250 g (9 oz) snow peas (mangetout)

60 ml (2 fl oz/¼ cup) oil

4 spring onions (scallions), cut into short
 lengths

1 tablespoon Chinese rice wine or dry
 sherry

½ teaspoon sugar

125 ml (4 fl oz/½ cup) Beef stock (page 43)

3 teaspoons cornflour (cornstarch)

Partially freeze the beef and slice it very thinly, then continue slicing into shreds. Place in a bowl with the soy sauce and salt, toss to coat and leave to marinate for at least 30 minutes.

Soak the mushrooms in hot water for 20–30 minutes, then drain well. Cut off and discard the mushroom stems and thinly slice the caps. Set aside.

Blanch the snow peas in a saucepan of boiling water for 2 minutes, then drain.

Heat 2 tablespoons of the oil in a wok or large heavy-based frying pan over high heat. Add the beef and stir-fry until it changes colour. Remove to a plate.

Heat the remaining oil in a clean wok over high heat. Add the mushroom and the spring onion and stir-fry for 1 minute, then add the rice wine, sugar and stock and bring to the boil.

In a small bowl, combine the cornflour and 1 tablespoon cold water and stir to make a smooth paste. Add to the wok and stir constantly until the sauce clears and thickens. Return the beef to the wok, add the snow peas and toss to combine and heat through. Serve immediately with rice or noodles.

See Yo Ngau Yook
Red-cooked beef

Serves 4–6

Here is how to use an economy cut of beef to make a superbly spiced, really special dish. Cooked in a master sauce, it makes a silk purse out of a sow's ear! Serve hot, or let it cool in the sauce, slice thinly and serve cold.

....

1.5 kg (3 lb 5 oz) beef shin (shank) in one piece

375 ml (12½ fl oz/1½ cups) dark soy sauce

60 ml (2 fl oz/¼ cup) Chinese rice wine or dry sherry

6 large slices fresh ginger

2 whole garlic cloves, peeled

2 whole star anise

2 tablespoons sugar

1 tablespoon sesame oil

Put the beef in a saucepan just large enough to hold it. Add all the remaining ingredients and 750 ml (25½ fl oz/3 cups) water, bring to the boil, then reduce the heat to low, cover, and simmer for 3 hours, turning the beef once or twice, so that it cooks evenly and is very tender. Test by piercing with a skewer, which should penetrate easily. Uncover the pan and cook for a further 15 minutes, spooning the sauce over the beef regularly.

You can either slice the beef and serve hot or allow the beef to cool in the sauce, turning it over after an hour. Chill until serving time, then cut into thin slices. Arrange overlapping slices as part of a selection of cold starters.

Note

You can reserve the cooking liquid, known as a master stock, freezing it for future use. A spoonful added to a dish in place of stock will give a rich, delicious flavour.

Doong Gwoo Chow Ngau Yook
Stir-fried beef with onions and mushrooms

Serves: 4

250 g (9 oz) lean rump (round) or fillet
  steak

6 dried shiitake mushrooms

¼ teaspoon Chinese five-spice

½ teaspoon salt

1 garlic clove, crushed

½ teaspoon finely grated fresh ginger

60 ml (2 fl oz/¼ cup) oil

2 onions, chopped

2 tablespoons dark soy sauce

2 teaspoons sugar

60 ml (2 fl oz/¼ cup) water or Beef stock
  (page 43)

2 teaspoons cornflour (cornstarch)

2 tablespoons thinly sliced spring onion
  (scallion) to garnish

Trim any fat from the beef, then freeze the beef for 1 hour or just until firm enough to cut into paper-thin slices.

Soak the mushrooms in hot water for 20–30 minutes, then drain well. Cut off and discard the mushroom stems and thinly slice the caps. Set aside.

In a bowl, combine the five-spice, salt, garlic and ginger. Add the beef and toss to coat.

Heat 1 tablespoon of the oil in a wok or large heavy-based frying pan over high heat. Add the mushroom and onion and stir-fry for 2–3 minutes, then add the beef and stir-fry until it changes colour. Add the soy sauce, sugar and water and bring to the boil.

In a small bowl, combine the cornflour and 1 tablespoon cold water and stir to make a smooth paste. Add to the wok and stir constantly until the sauce thickens. Serve immediately, garnished with the spring onion.

Seen Lo Shun Chow Ngau Yook
Stir-fried beef with fresh asparagus

Serves: 4–6

375 g (13 oz) lean rump (round) or fillet
  steak

2 teaspoons light soy sauce

1 garlic clove, crushed with ½ teaspoon salt

80 ml (2½ fl oz/⅓ cup) peanut oil

12 asparagus spears, sliced diagonally,
  separating spears and tips

2 onions, chopped

2 teaspoons Chinese ground bean sauce

60 ml (2 fl oz/¼ cup) water or Beef stock
  (page 43)

1 teaspoon cornflour (cornstarch)

Trim any fat from the beef, then freeze the beef for 1 hour or just until firm enough to cut into paper-thin slices.

In a bowl, combine the soy sauce and garlic. Add the beef and toss to coat. Set aside.

Heat 2 tablespoons of the peanut oil in a wok or large heavy-based frying pan over high heat. Add the meat and stir-fry until it changes colour. Remove to a plate.

Heat the remaining oil in a clean wok over high heat. Add the asparagus spears and stir-fry for 3 minutes, then add the onion and stir-fry for a further 1 minute. Add the bean sauce and water, and stir to combine, then add the asparagus tips. Reduce the heat, cover and simmer until the asparagus is tender but not mushy.

In a small bowl, combine the cornflour and 1 tablespoon cold water and stir to make a smooth paste. Push the vegetables to one side of the wok and add the cornflour paste, stirring constantly until the sauce boils and thickens. Return the beef to the wok and stir gently to combine and heat through. Serve immediately with white rice.

Yook Nup Fun See
Cellophane noodles with pork

Serves: 4–6

125 g (4½ oz) cellophane (bean thread) noodles

4 dried shiitake mushrooms

1 tablespoon Chinese rice wine or dry sherry

1 tablespoon light soy sauce

1 teaspoon salt

190 ml (6½ fl oz/¾ cup) light stock (page 42) or water

1 teaspoon cornflour (cornstarch)

60 ml (2 fl oz/¼ cup) oil

185 g (6½ oz) pork fillet (tenderloin), diced

4 spring onions (scallions), thinly sliced

2 teaspoons finely grated fresh ginger

2 tablespoons Chinese ground bean sauce

1 large fresh red chilli, deseeded and chopped

2 tablespoons chopped fresh coriander (cilantro) leaves

Soak the noodles in boiling water for 5 minutes, then drain and cut into short lengths. Set aside.

Soak the mushrooms in hot water for 20–30 minutes, then drain well. Cut off and discard the mushroom stems and thinly slice the caps. Set aside.

In a bowl, combine the rice wine, soy sauce, salt, stock and cornflour. Set aside.

Heat the oil in a wok or large heavy-based frying pan over high heat. Add the pork and mushroom and stir-fry until the pork is cooked and brown. Add the spring onion and ginger, stir-fry for a few seconds, then add the bean sauce and chilli and cook over medium heat for 1–2 minutes, or until well combined and cooked through.

Add the soy sauce mixture and stir to combine. Bring to the boil, then add the noodles, reduce the heat to low and simmer, stirring until all the liquid has reduced. Stir in the coriander leaves and serve immediately.

Note

In Sichuan tradition, this dish is seasoned with hot bean sauce. If this is not available substitute it with 2 tablespoons rinsed and drained salted yellow beans. Mash them in a bowl and stir in 2 teaspoons Chinese chilli sauce before adding to the dish.

Ngau Yook Dau Kok Chow Mi Fun

Rice vermicelli with beef and long beans

Serves: 4–5

375 g (13 oz) lean rump (round) or fillet steak

250 g (9 oz) rice vermicelli (rice-stick) noodles

1 tablespoon peanut oil

375 g (13 oz) snake (yard-long) beans, cut into 5 cm (2 in) lengths

1 garlic clove, crushed

½ teaspoon finely grated fresh ginger

250 ml (8½ fl oz/1 cup) Beef stock (page 43)

1 teaspoon salt

2 tablespoons light soy sauce

chilli oil to serve (optional)

Trim any fat from the beef, then freeze the beef for 1 hour or just until firm enough to cut into paper-thin slices.

Soak the vermicelli noodles in hot water for 10 minutes, then drain.

Heat the peanut oil in a wok or large heavy-based frying pan over medium heat. Add the beans and stir-fry for 2 minutes, then remove to a plate.

Add the garlic, ginger and beef to the wok and stir-fry until the beef changes colour. Add the stock, salt, soy sauce and rice vermicelli and toss until heated through. Cover and cook over low heat for 3 minutes, then return the beans to the wok, toss to combine and heat through, then serve immediately with the chilli oil, if using, passed separately.

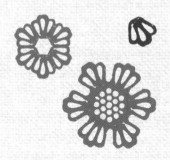

Meat

Vegetables

*

Chu Hau Jeung Mun Wan Yee
Wood ears in hoisin sauce

Serves: 4

10 g (¼ oz/½ cup) dried wood ear fungus

2 teaspoons hoisin sauce

2 tablespoons light soy sauce

2 teaspoons peanut oil

1 teaspoon sesame oil

1 small garlic clove, crushed

1 teaspoon cornflour (cornstarch)

Wash the wood ear fungus, then drain and place in a bowl with enough hot water to cover and leave to soak for 1 hour. The wood ear fungus will swell to many times its original size. Rinse well and cut off any thick or gritty parts, then chop any large pieces.

In a bowl, mix together the hoisin sauce and soy sauce.

Heat the peanut and sesame oils in a wok or large heavy-based frying pan over low heat. Add the garlic and stir-fry for 30 seconds, then add the combined sauces, 60 ml (2 fl oz/¼ cup) water and the wood ear fungus and bring to the boil. In a small bowl combine the cornflour and 1 tablespoon cold water and stir to make a smooth paste. Add to the wok and stir until the sauce thickens. Serve immediately with rice or noodles.

Chu Hau Jeung Mun Dau Fu
Tofu in barbecue sauce

Serves: 4–6

2 tablespoons oil

530 g (1 lb 3 oz) firm tofu, drained

2 tablespoons Chinese barbecue (char siu) sauce

190 ml (6½ fl oz/¾ cup) light stock (page 42) or water

155 g (5½ oz/1 cup) cooked peas or thinly sliced spring onion (scallion)

Heat the oil in a wok or large heavy-based frying pan over high heat. Add the tofu and cook for 3–4 minutes, turning once. Mix the barbecue sauce and stock together, then add to the wok and simmer for 3 minutes. Add the peas and heat through. Serve with boiled rice or noodles.

Vegetables ❀

Hung Shiu Doong Gwoo
Braised mushrooms

Serves: 6–8

125 g (4½ oz) dried shiitake mushrooms

2 tablespoons dark soy sauce

2 tablespoons sugar

1 tablespoon sesame oil

60 ml (2 fl oz/¼ cup) peanut oil

Note

Braised mushrooms can also be added to other dishes, either whole or sliced.

Soak the mushrooms in 1 litre (34 fl oz/4 cups) hot water for 20–30 minutes, then drain well, reserving the soaking liquid. Cut off and discard the mushroom stems.

In a bowl, combine 375 ml (12½ fl oz/1½ cups) of the reserved soaking liquid with the soy sauce, sugar and sesame oil, stirring to dissolve the sugar.

Heat the peanut oil in a wok or large heavy-based frying pan over high heat. Add the mushrooms and cook for 3 minutes, turning and pressing both sides until brown on both sides. Add the sauce mixture and bring to the boil, then reduce the heat to low, cover, and simmer for about 30 minutes, stirring towards the end of the cooking time, until all the liquid is absorbed and the mushrooms take on a shiny appearance. Serve hot or cold.

Hai Yook Par Dau Fu
Tofu with crab sauce

Serves: 4

2 tablespoons peanut oil

6 spring onions (scallions), sliced

½ teaspoon finely grated fresh ginger

190 ml (6½ fl oz/¾ cup) Chicken or Fish stock (page 42)

155 g (5½ oz/¾ cup) crabmeat

2½ teaspoons cornflour (cornstarch)

530 g (1 lb 3 oz) firm tofu, drained and cut into quarters

Heat the oil in a small saucepan over medium heat. Add the spring onion and ginger and cook until the ginger and onion are soft. Add the stock, cover, and simmer for 3–4 minutes, then add the crabmeat and heat through.

In a bowl, combine the cornflour and 1 tablespoon cold water and stir to make a smooth paste. Add to the pan, season with freshly ground black pepper, and stir until the sauce boils and thickens. Add the tofu and heat through until the sauce almost returns to the boil – do not overcook. Serve immediately with rice.

Jilng Yeung Buck Gwoo
Steamed mushrooms with pork filling

Makes: about 24

250 g (9 oz) fresh button mushrooms

250 g (9 oz) minced (ground) pork

6 water chestnuts, finely chopped

1 tablespoon cornflour (cornstarch), plus
   1 teaspoon extra

1 tablespoon light soy sauce

¾ teaspoon salt

½ teaspoon finely grated fresh ginger

½ teaspoon sugar

sesame oil

fresh coriander (cilantro) leaves to garnish

Wipe the mushrooms with damp paper towel, then carefully remove and discard the stems, leaving the caps intact.

In a bowl, combine the pork, water chestnuts, cornflour, soy sauce, salt, ginger and sugar. Put a teaspoonful of the mixture into each mushroom cap, pressing it firmly to create a slight mound shape.

Lightly grease a heatproof dish with a little sesame oil and arrange the mushrooms in the base. Cover with foil, and steam the mushrooms over simmering water for 25–30 minutes. Remove the mushrooms to a serving dish. If the mushrooms are being served as appetisers, save the flavoursome liquid in the base of the dish for adding to soups or sauces. If the mushrooms are to be eaten as part of a meal, thicken the liquid slightly by adding more stock or water to make 190 ml (6½ fl oz/¾ cup); bring to the boil in a small saucepan.

In a small bowl, combine the extra cornflour and 2 tablespoons cold water and stir to make a smooth paste. Add to the stock and stir until the sauce boils and thickens. Pour the sauce over the warm mushrooms and serve with white rice.

Lo Han Chai

Braised vegetable combination

Serves: 6

....

125 g (4½ oz) dried tofu or dried soya bean
    protein (glossary)

12 dried shiitake mushrooms

30 dried lily buds (golden needles)

2 tablespoons dried wood ear fungus

60 ml (2 fl oz/¼ cup) peanut oil

2 tablespoons light soy sauce

2 tablespoons hoisin sauce

3 segments star anise

1 tinned bamboo shoot, thinly sliced

1 frozen lotus root, thinly sliced

90 g (3 oz) ginkgo nuts or water chestnuts
    (optional)

2 teaspoons sesame oil

2 teaspoons sugar

2 teaspoons cornflour (cornstarch)

Soak the dried tofu in cold water for 20 minutes. Drain, then place in a bowl, pour boiling water over and leave to soak for 20 minutes. Drain well. Soak the mushrooms in hot water for 20–30 minutes, then drain well, reserving 375 ml (12½ fl oz/1½ cups) of the soaking liquid. Cut off and discard the mushroom stems. Soak the lily buds in hot water for 30 minutes, drain, pinch off the tough stem ends and cut into halves. Soak the wood ear fungus in hot water for 10 minutes, drain and cut into bite-sized pieces, discarding any gritty or thick bits.

Heat the peanut oil in a wok or large heavy-based frying pan over medium heat. Add the tofu, mushrooms and lily buds and stir-fry for 4 minutes, then add the combined soy and hoisin sauces and some of the reserved soaking liquid. Add the star anise, bring to the boil, then reduce the heat to low, cover, and simmer for 15 minutes. Add the bamboo shoot, lotus root, ginkgo nuts, sesame oil and sugar, stir well, cover and simmer for a further 10 minutes, adding more soaking liquid if needed. In a small bowl, combine the cornflour and 2 tablespoons cold water to make a smooth paste and add to the wok, stirring until the sauce thickens. Push the vegetables to the side of the wok and add the wood ear fungus, allowing it to heat through. Serve hot with rice.

Par Say Saw
Mixed braised vegetables

Serves: 4–6

....

2 tablespoons peanut oil

1 teaspoon sesame oil

1 large garlic clove, crushed

1 teaspoon grated fresh ginger

750 g (1 lb 11 oz) sliced vegetables

125 ml (4 fl oz/½ cup) hot water or light
    stock (page 42)

1 tablespoon oyster sauce

2 teaspoons light soy sauce

½ teaspoon salt

2 teaspoons cornflour (cornstarch)

Heat the peanut and sesame oils in a wok or large heavy-based frying pan over high heat. Add the garlic, ginger and vegetables and stir-fry for 2 minutes. Add the hot water, then the combined oyster and soy sauces and salt. Cover and simmer for 4 minutes. In a bowl, combine the cornflour and 1 tablespoon cold water and stir to make a smooth paste. Push the vegetables to one side of the wok and add the cornflour paste, stirring until the sauce thickens. Toss the vegetables to coat and serve immediately with white rice.

Chow Dau Kok
Quick-fried long beans

Serves: 4

....

2 tablespoons peanut oil

1 garlic clove, crushed

½ teaspoon finely grated fresh ginger

500 g (1 lb 2 oz) snake (yard-long) beans,
    trimmed and cut into 5 cm (2 in) lengths

1 teaspoon sesame oil

½ teaspoon salt

Heat the oil in a wok or large heavy-based frying pan over high heat. Add the garlic, ginger and beans and stir-fry for 2 minutes, or until the beans are tender but still crunchy. Stir in the sesame oil and salt and serve immediately.

Chow Sahng Choy
Braised lettuce

Serves: 2–4

....

1 tablespoon peanut oil

1 small garlic clove, crushed

¼ teaspoon finely grated fresh ginger

1 large firm head of iceberg lettuce, leaves
  separated and chopped

2 tablespoons light stock (page 42) or water

1 teaspoon sugar

2 teaspoons light soy sauce

1 teaspoon cornflour (cornstarch)

Heat the peanut oil in a wok or large heavy-based frying pan over high heat. Add the garlic, ginger and lettuce and stir-fry for 1 minute, then add the stock, sugar, soy sauce and a pinch of salt. In a bowl, combine the cornflour and 1 tablespoon cold water and stir to make a smooth paste. Push the lettuce to one side of the wok and add the cornflour paste, stirring until the sauce boils and thickens. Toss to coat the lettuce in the sauce and serve immediately.

Jun Ju Shun Ho Lan Dau Chang Gwa
Corn and snow peas with cucumber

Serves: 4

....

1 tablespoon peanut oil

1 teaspoon sesame oil

½ teaspoon crushed garlic

½ teaspoon finely grated fresh ginger

440 g (15½ oz) tinned baby corn, rinsed and
  drained

250 g (9 oz) snow peas (mangetout),
  trimmed

1 cucumber, peeled and thinly sliced

Heat the peanut and sesame oils in a wok or large heavy-based frying pan over high heat. Add the garlic and ginger and cook for 30 seconds, then add the corn and snow peas and stir-fry for 1 minute. Add the cucumber and stir-fry a further 2 minutes, or until translucent. Serve immediately.

Hung Shiu Say Saw
Heavenly braised vegetables

Serves: 4

12 dried shiitake mushrooms

3 tablespoons dried wood ear fungus

2 tablespoons peanut oil

1 tablespoon sesame oil

250 g (9 oz/1 cup) tinned bamboo shoots, rinsed, drained and thinly sliced

425 g (15 oz) tinned whole baby corn, rinsed and drained

2 tablespoons soy sauce

1 tablespoon sugar

Soak the mushrooms in hot water for 20–30 minutes, then drain well, reserving 500 ml (17 fl oz/2 cups) of the soaking liquid. Cut off and discard the mushroom stems and thinly slice the caps. Soak the wood ear fungus in hot water for 10 minutes, then drain and halve, removing any thick or gritty bits.

Heat the peanut and sesame oils in a wok or large heavy-based frying pan over medium heat. Add the mushroom and stir-fry for 5 minutes, or until brown. Add the bamboo shoots, corn, soy sauce, sugar and reserved soaking liquid. Cover and simmer over low heat for 20–30 minutes. Add the wood ear fungus and heat through. Serve immediately with rice.

Jahp Sik Choy
Chinese salad

Serves: 4–6

Salads are rare in Chinese cuisine, but they do exist. Here is a delicious combination that may be served as a vegetable accompaniment or as a main dish.

½ head Chinese cabbage (wombok), finely shredded

550 g (1 lb 4 oz) tinned winter bamboo shoots, drained and thinly sliced (see note)

390 g (14 oz/4⅓ cups) fresh bean sprouts, trimmed

370 g (13 oz/2 cups) peeled fresh or tinned lychees (optional)

2 tablespoons lightly toasted sesame seeds

Dressing

1 teaspoon finely grated fresh ginger

1 garlic clove, crushed

1½ teaspoons salt

1 tablespoon light soy sauce

2 tablespoons Chinese rice wine or dry sherry

80 ml (2½ fl oz/⅓ cup) sweet Chinese vinegar or other mild vinegar

125 ml (4 fl oz/½ cup) peanut oil

2 tablespoons sesame oil

Put the cabbage in a large serving bowl and arrange the winter bamboo shoots and bean sprouts on top. Pile the lychees in the centre, if using, and sprinkle over the sesame seeds. Cover with plastic wrap and chill until serving time.

To make the dressing, combine all the ingredients in a bowl. Just before serving, pour over the salad and toss to combine. Serve immediately.

Note

Winter bamboo shoots are smaller, whiter and much more tender than ordinary bamboo shoots. If they are not available use the larger variety but after slicing, bring to the boil in lightly salted water, simmer for 8 minutes, then drain and cool.

Vegetables ❁

See Jup Yeung Fu Gwa
Stuffed bitter melon in black bean sauce

Serves: 2–3

2 bitter melons (gourds)

375 g (13 oz) boneless skinless bream (porgy) fillet, chopped

125 g (4½ oz) raw prawns (shrimp), peeled, deveined and chopped

¾ teaspoon salt

1 teaspoon finely grated fresh ginger

1 tablespoon egg white

1 teaspoon cornflour (cornstarch)

80 ml (2½ fl oz/⅓ cup) peanut oil

Sauce

2 tablespoons tinned salted black beans, rinsed and drained

1 garlic clove, crushed

1 teaspoon sugar

125 ml (4 fl oz/½ cup) light stock (page 42) or water

1½ teaspoons cornflour (cornstarch)

Trim the bitter melons and cut into 4 cm (1½ in) thick slices. With a small sharp knife, remove the spongy centre, leaving small tubular shells of melon.

In a bowl, mix together the fish, prawn meat, salt, ginger, egg white and cornflour. Spoon this mixture into the melon shells, rounding the filling slightly on one end.

Heat the peanut oil in a wok or large heavy-based frying pan over medium heat. Add the melon, round side down, and cook for 8 minutes, or until the filling just starts to brown. Turn over and cook the other side. Remove to a plate once cooked, reserving the oil in the wok for making the sauce.

To make the sauce, mash the black beans with a fork and mix together with the garlic. Add to the reserved oil in the wok and cook over medium heat, stirring well. Add the sugar and stock and bring to the boil. Return the melon to the wok, round side up, cover and simmer over low heat for 20 minutes. Remove the melon to a serving plate.

In a bowl, combine the cornflour and 1 tablespoon cold water and stir to make a smooth paste. Add to the wok and stir until the sauce boils and thickens. Pour over the stuffed bitter melon and serve immediately with white rice.

Accompaniments

*

See Yau Ghung Jeung
Ginger soy sauce

Makes: 165 ml (5½ fl oz)

Serve with fried or stir-fried seafood or steamed dumplings.

1 teaspoon finely grated fresh ginger

125 ml (4 fl oz/½ cup) light soy sauce

In a bowl, combine the ginger and soy sauce. The sauce can be prepared in advance and stored in an airtight container in the refrigerator for up to 1 week.

See Yau Laht Jiu Jeung
Chilli-soy sauce

Makes: 80 ml (2½ fl oz/⅓ cup)

This sauce is best served with fried prawns (shrimp), dim sum or hot or cold appetisers.

2 tablespoons Chinese chilli sauce

125 ml (4 fl oz/½ cup) soy sauce

In a bowl, combine the chilli sauce and soy sauce. The sauce can be prepared in advance and stored in an airtight container in the refrigerator indefinitely.

Dau See Sheung Jing Jeung
Black bean sherry sauce

Makes: 125 ml (4 fl oz/½ cup)

This sauce is subtle enough to be served with delicate seafood dishes, such as crab and scallops.

1 tablespoon tinned salted black beans, rinsed and drained

60 ml (2 fl oz/¼ cup) Chinese rice wine or dry sherry

1 teaspoon sugar

a few drops of sesame oil

Use a fork to mash the black beans in a bowl to make a chunky paste, then stir to combine with the rice wine, sugar and just enough sesame oil to make a runny sauce.

Suen Tau Dau See
Black bean garlic sauce

Makes: 125 ml (4 fl oz/½ cup)

Serve this sauce with rich meats, such as pork or duck.

2 tablespoons tinned salted black beans, rinsed and drained

1 garlic clove, crushed

2 tablespoons light soy sauce

2 tablespoons Chinese rice wine or dry sherry

Use a fork to mash the black beans in a bowl to make a chunky paste, then stir in the remaining ingredients until well combined.

Tim Suen Jeung
Sweet sour sauce

Makes: 250 ml (8½ fl oz/1 cup)

Serve with hot appetisers or fried won tons.

1 tablespoon light soy sauce

1 tablespoon Chinese rice wine or dry sherry (optional)

60 ml (2 fl oz/¼ cup) tomato sauce (ketchup)

2 tablespoons white vinegar

2 tablespoons white sugar

1 tablespoon cornflour (cornstarch)

2 tablespoons peanut oil

1 garlic clove, crushed

¼ teaspoon finely grated fresh ginger

1 small onion, cut into large chunks and layers separated

1 teaspoon Chinese chilli sauce (optional)

In a bowl, combine the soy sauce, rice wine, tomato sauce, vinegar, sugar and 190 ml (6½ fl oz/¾ cup) water, stirring until the sugar has dissolved.

In a separate bowl, combine the cornflour and 1 tablespoon cold water and stir to make a smooth paste. Set aside.

Heat the peanut oil in a saucepan over medium heat. Add the garlic, ginger and onion and cook for 1 minute. Add the soy sauce mixture, bring to the boil, then add the cornflour paste and stir constantly until the sauce boils and thickens. Remove from the heat and stir in the chilli sauce, if using. Serve warm.

Tim Suen Jeung
Sweet sour pickle sauce

Makes: about 500 ml (17 fl oz/2 cups)

This tangy sauce is ideal to serve with deep-fried meats or vegetables.

140 g (5 oz/½ cup) tinned Chinese pickles, reserving 80 ml (2½ fl oz/⅓ cup) liquid

80 g (2¾ oz/½ cup) tinned pineapple pieces, reserving 80 ml (2½ fl oz/⅓ cup) syrup

80 ml (2½ fl oz/⅓ cup) white vinegar

a pinch of red food colouring powder (glossary) (optional)

2 tablespoons sugar

½ teaspoon salt

1 small garlic clove, crushed

3 teaspoons cornflour (cornstarch)

Cut the pickles into pieces, then place in a bowl with the pineapple pieces and set aside.

Put the reserved liquid from both the pickles and pineapple into a small enamel saucepan with the vinegar, red colouring powder, if using, the sugar, salt and garlic. Bring to the boil, then reduce the heat to low and simmer for 2 minutes. Add the pickle and pineapple pieces and return to the boil briefly.

In a bowl, combine the cornflour and 2 tablespoons cold water and stir to make a smooth paste. Add to the pan and stir constantly until the sauce has thickened and is clear.

Goo Yuet Fun Yim
Roasted pepper and salt mix

2 tablespoons whole black peppercorns

3 teaspoons salt

Heat the peppercorns in a dry frying pan over medium heat for 4–5 minutes, shaking the pan or stirring, until the peppercorns are aromatic. Remove from the pan, allow to cool slightly, then pound using a mortar and pestle and stir in the salt. Store in an airtight container.

Soo Mui Jeung, Shiu Hau Ieung
Plum and barbecue sauce

Makes: about 300 ml (10 fl oz)

This sauce is excellent served with roast duck or barbecued pork dishes.

125 ml (4 fl oz/½ cup) plum sauce

125 ml (4 fl oz/½ cup) Chinese barbecue (char siu) sauce

½ teaspoon ginger juice, extracted from fresh ginger

2 tablespoons light soy sauce

1 teaspoon Chinese chilli sauce to taste (optional)

Put all the ingredients in a bowl and stir well to combine. The sauce can be prepared in advance and stored in an airtight container in the refrigerator indefinitely.

Wah Yim
Salt and five-spice mix

Rather than a sauce, this spiced salt combination can be sprinkled over crisp-fried chicken, roasted duck or pork.

2 tablespoons salt

1 teaspoon Chinese five-spice

In a bowl, mix together the salt and five-spice until well combined. Serve in a small bowl and let guests sprinkle over their meal as desired.

Sweets
and
Desserts

✳

Hung Yun Dau Fu
Almond tofu

Serves: 6–8

This lightly sweetened milk dessert is so named because of its resemblance to tofu.

1 tablespoon agar-agar powder

390 ml (13 fl oz) tinned sweetened
condensed milk

2 teaspoons natural almond extract

Put 1 litre (34 fl oz/4 cups) water into a saucepan and sprinkle over the agar-agar powder, then bring to the boil, stirring until the agar-agar has dissolved. Add the condensed milk and almond extract and stir well to combine. Pour the mixture into a large shallow glass dish. Allow to cool, then refrigerate for about 30 minutes to set. Cut into cubes or diamond shapes and serve by itself or with tinned fruit or melon balls.

Doong Fong Sik Gow Lahm
Oriental fruit basket

Serves: 8–10

1 watermelon

555 g (1 lb 4 oz/3 cups) tinned lychees,
rinsed and drained, reserving the syrup

4 mandarins, broken into segments, white
pith removed

500 g (1 lb 2 oz) longans or loquats, peeled
and deseeded

200 g (7 oz) bottled chow chow preserves,
drained and diced (optional)

Cut off the top third of the watermelon and use a melon-baller to scoop out the flesh in neat balls. Combine the melon balls in a bowl with the lychees, mandarin segments and longans. Stir in just enough lychee syrup to coat the fruit, then cover and refrigerate for at least 3 hours.

Use a knife to scallop the edge of the watermelon shell. Before serving, arrange the fruit in the watermelon shell and spoon some of the remaining syrup over the top. If liked, you can serve with the chow chow preserves, which will add extra texture and flavour.

Jar Won Ton
Deep-fried sweet won tons

Makes: about 50

270 g (9½ oz/1½ cups) pitted dates, finely chopped

60 g (2 oz/½ cup) chopped walnuts, cashew nuts or almonds

finely grated zest of 1 large lemon

1 tablespoon orange juice

300 g (10½ oz) won ton wrappers

peanut oil for deep-frying

icing (confectioners') sugar for dusting

Note

You can make these won tons using tinned lotus nut filling instead of the dates and nuts.

In a bowl, combine the dates, walnuts, lemon zest and orange juice and mix thoroughly, adding more orange juice if the mixture is too dry – it needs to hold together and this will depend on the quality of the dates. Form the date mixture into small cylinders, about 5 cm (2 in) long, with a 2 cm (¾ in) diameter.

Lay the won ton wrappers out on a clean work surface and place a date cylinder over each, positioning it closer to one corner. Starting from the filled end, roll up each wrapper to enclose the filling and twist the ends to seal. Repeat until all the won ton wrappers and filling are used.

Heat the peanut oil in a wok or large heavy-based frying pan over medium heat. Gently lower the won tons into the hot oil and deep-fry, in batches, for about 2 minutes, turning once, until they are golden brown all over. Remove the won tons using a slotted spoon and drain on paper towel. Allow to cool and dust with icing sugar before serving.

Glossary
and Index

*

Agar-Agar

A setting agent obtained from seaweed, agar-agar is widely used in Asia, as it sets without refrigeration. It is sold in sachets in powder form and is available from Asian grocery stores and health food stores. It is also sold in strands, though they are less obtainable and slower to dissolve. Also known as: *dai choy goh* (China); *kanten* (Japan); *kyauk kyaw* (Burma); *chun chow* (Sri Lanka); *rau cau,* (Vietnam).

Bamboo Shoots

Sold in tins and jars, either water-packed, pickled or braised. Unless otherwise stated, the recipes in this book use the water-packed variety. If using the tinned variety, store leftover bamboo shoots in a bowl of fresh water in the refrigerator, changing the water daily for up to 10 days. Winter bamboo shoots are much smaller and more tender, and are called for in certain recipes; however, if they are not available, use the larger variety. Also known as: *suehn* (China); *takenoko* (Japan); *rebong* (Malaysia); *rebung* (Indonesia); (Vietnam).

Barbecue (Char Siu) Sauce

A reddish sauce, *char siu* is very salty and at the same time heavily sweetened. Use as a dip or as an ingredient in barbecue marinades. Keeps indefinitely in an airtight jar.

Bean Sprouts

Green mung beans are traditionally used for bean sprouts. They are sold fresh in most large supermarkets, Asian grocery stores and health food stores. Chinese stores sell longer shoots than those available from supermarkets, which are usually just starting to sprout. Substitute thinly sliced celery for a similar texture but different flavour. Very fresh bean sprouts can be stored in the refrigerator for up to 4 days in a plastic bag; alternatively, cover with water and change the water daily. Before using, rinse the sprouts, drain well and trim off the brown tails.

Beni Shoga

Pickled ginger, coloured bright red, and sold in plastic packets or in bottles. Used as a garnish or for flavour.

Bitter Gourd (Bitter Melon)

Botanical name: *Momordica charantia*

Known variously as bitter melon, bitter gourd, bitter cucumber and balsam pear, this vaguely reptilian-looking vegetable with warty green exterior should be purchased while young and shiny-skinned. Do not store more than a day or two and even then, in the refrigerator, or it will continue to mature. Over-ripe specimens will yellow and their seeds will become very hard. Cultures all over Asia believe this vegetable has powerful medicinal benefits. Also known as: *fu gwa, foo kwa* (China); *karela* (India); *karavila* (Sri Lanka); *niga-uri* (Japan); *pare, peria* (Indonesia); *peria* (Malaysia); *kho qua* (Vietnam); *bai maha* (Laos); *mara* (Thailand); *ampalaya* (The Philippines).

Black Beans, Salted

Made from soy beans, heavily salted and sold in tins and jars. Rinse before using to avoid over-salting recipes. Substitute extra soy sauce for flavour, though not for appearance. Store in an airtight jar in the refrigerator after opening — it will keep for 6 months or longer. Pour a little peanut oil over it if the top seems to dry out. Also known as: *dow see* (China).

Cellophane (Bean Starch) Noodles

Fine, translucent noodles made from the starch of green mung beans. Noodles may be soaked in hot water before use, or may require boiling according to the texture required. They can also be deep-fried straight from the packet, generally when used as a garnish or to provide a background for other foods. Also known as: *kyazan* (Burma); *woon sen* (Thailand); *sohoon, tunghoon* (Malaysia); *bi fun, ning fun, sai fun, fun see* (China); *harusame* (Japan); *sotanghoon* (Indonesia); *sotanghon* (The Philippines); *búng u* (Vietnam); *mee sooer* (Cambodia).

Chilli Powder

Asian chilli powder is made from ground chillies. It is much hotter than the Mexican-style chilli powder, which is mostly ground cumin. You may be able to find ground Kashmiri chillies, which are a brighter red colour and not as hot as other ground chillies.

Chillies, Green And Red

Botanical name: *Capsicum spp.*

Chillies mature from green to red, becoming hotter as they mature. Both varieties are used fresh for flavouring, either whole or finely chopped, sliced as a garnish or ground into sambals. The seeds, which are the hottest parts, are usually (though not always) removed. Larger varieties tend to be milder than the small varieties. See page 7 for handling. Dried red chillies are found in packets in Asian grocery stores — the medium- to large-sized chillies are best for most recipes in this book.

Chinese Bean Sauce

Most bean sauces are too thick to pour, they are a paste consistency. There are many types of bean sauce — each country has at least one used in its cuisine. In Chinese cooking, ground bean sauce (*mor sze jeung*) has a smooth texture and can be used as a substitute for Korean bean sauce in cooking. Another type, *min sze jeung*, is a thick paste of mashed fermented soy beans and is similar to Malaysian taucheo. Whenever bean sauce is an ingredient in recipes from Malaysia, Singapore and China, use *min sze jeung* if possible. Substitute mashed salted black beans, sold in tins. Other variations include Chinese chilli bean sauce, sweet bean sauce and hot bean sauce.

Chinese Sausages

Known as *lap cheong,* these dried sausages are filled only with spiced lean and fat pork. Steam for 10–15 minutes until soft and plump and the fat is translucent. Cut into thin slices to serve, or include in other dishes. They have a sweet, lightly scented flavour that can be an acquired taste.

Chow Chow Preserves

A mixture of fruits and vegetables in a heavy syrup, flavoured with ginger, which is also one of the ingredients. Sold in tins or jars, it keeps indefinitely in the refrigerator after opening.

Coriander

Botanical name: *Coriandrum sativum*

Family name: *Umbelliferae*

All parts of the coriander plant are used in Asian cooking. The dried seed is the main ingredient in curry powder, and although not hot it has a fragrance that makes it an essential part of a curry blend. The fresh coriander herb is also known as cilantro or Chinese parsley in other parts of the world. It is indispensable in Burma, Thailand, Vietnam, Cambodia, India and China where it is also called 'fragrant green'. Also known as: *dhania* (seed), *dhania pattar, dhania sabz* (leaves) (India); *kottamalli* (seed), *kottamalli kolle* (leaves) (Sri Lanka); *nannamzee* (seed), *nannambin* (leaves) (Burma); *pak chee* (Thailand); *phak hom pom* (Laos); *ketumbar* (seeds), *daun ketumbar* (leaves) (Malaysia); *yuen sai* (China); *kinchay* (The Philippines); *ngò, rau mùi* (Vietnam); *chee van soy* (Cambodia).

Daikon
Botanical name: *Raphanus sativus*

This is a very large white radish most popularly known by its Japanese name and it is about 30–38 cm long with a mild flavour. It is sold in Asian grocery stores and some large greengrocers and supermarkets. Substitute white turnip if not available. Also known as: *muuli* (India); *loh hahk* (China); *cù cùi trng* (Vietnam); *mu (moo)* (Korea).

Dow Foo Pok
Chinese-style fried bean curd, sold in Asian grocery stores. It comes in small or large cubes and is sold fresh, not frozen, but can be kept in the refrigerator for about a week.

Fish Cakes
Both Chinese-style fish cakes and Japanese-style fish cakes are sold ready to use in most Asian grocery stores. They can be kept for a few days if refrigerated, and need no further cooking apart from heating through.

Five-Spice Powder
Essential in Chinese cooking, this reddish-brown powder is a combination of ground star anise, fennel, cinnamon, cloves and sichuan pepper. Also known as: *heung new fun, hung liu, ngung heung fun* (China).

Ginger
Botanical name: *Zingiber officinale*

A rhizome with a robust flavour and a warming quality, it is essential in most Asian dishes. Fresh ginger root should be used; powdered ginger cannot be substituted for fresh ginger, for the flavour is quite different. To prepare for use, scrape off the skin with a sharp knife and either grate or chop finely (according to recipe requirements) before measuring. To preserve fresh ginger for long periods of time, place in a freezer bag and store in the freezer — it is a simple matter to peel and grate in the frozen state. Also known as: *adrak* (India); *inguru* (Sri Lanka); *gin* (Burma); *khing* (Thailand); *khnyahee* (Cambodia); *halia* (Malaysia); *jahe* (Indonesia); *jeung* (China); *shoga* (Japan); (Vietnam); *luya* (The Philippines).

Ginkgo Nuts
Botanical name: *Ginkgo biloba*

Family name: *Ginkgoacea*

The kernel of the fruit of the maidenhair tree, which grows in China and Japan. It has an individual and slightly bitter flavour, and is eaten roasted as a nut or used to give its flavour to foods.

Usually sold tinned or shrink-sealed, it may also be labelled 'white nut'. Before eating, fresh nuts need to have their outer layer removed and then should be boiled for about 30 minutes or they can be toxic. The nut, or seed of the fruit in its shell, looks a little like a large, closed pistachio nut. Also known as: *bahk gwoah* (China); *ginnan* (Japan).

Hoisin Sauce
A sweet, spicy, reddish-brown sauce of thick pouring consistency made from soy beans, garlic and spices. Used in barbecued pork dishes and as a dip. Keeps indefinitely in an airtight jar.

Lily Buds
Botanical name: *Hemerocallis*

Also known as 'golden needles' or 'lotus buds', these long, narrow, dried golden buds have a very delicate flavour and are said to be nutritious. Before using, soak for 30 minutes or longer in hot water, then cut in half widthways or tie in a knot for more elegant eating. Also known as: *khim chiam* (China); *kanzou* (Japan); *pet kup julgi* (Korea); *dole mai chin* (Thailand); *kim cham* (Vietnam).

Lotus Root
Botanical name: *Nelumbo nucifera*

The edible rhizome of the graceful, ancient flowering water plant. Sometimes available fresh; peel, cut into slices and use as directed. Dried lotus root must be soaked for at least 20 minutes in hot water with a little lemon juice added to preserve whiteness. Peeled and sliced frozen lotus root is widely available. Tinned lotus root can be stored in the refrigerator for a few days after being opened. The seeds of the spent flower, peeled and eaten raw as a snack in Asia, are mild-tasting with a subtle crunch. Also known as: *kamal-kakri* (India); *nelun-ala* (Sri Lanka); *seroja* (Malaysia); *teratai* (Indonesia); *baino* (The Philippines); *bua-luang* (Thailand); *lien ngow, ngau* (China); *renkon* (Japan).

Melon, Bitter
See bitter gourd.

Mushrooms, Dried
See shiitake mushrooms, dried.

Mushrooms, Straw
Also known as 'paddy straw mushrooms'. Especially popular in Japan, this tiny, cultivated mushroom consists of a sheath within which is the mushroom. Available tinned, bottled or dried. Very delicate flavour. Substitute champignons. Also known as: *chao gwoo* (China), *nameko* (Japan).

Oyster Sauce
Adds delicate flavour to all kinds of dishes. Made from oysters cooked in soy sauce and brine, this thick brown sauce can be kept indefinitely in the refrigerator. Also known as: *ho yu* (China).

Peanut Oil
A traditional cooking medium in Chinese and Southeast Asian countries. Asian unrefined peanut oil is highly flavoured and more expensive than the refined peanut oil found in Western supermarkets. It has a high smoking point and adds a distinctive flavour to stir-fries. Refined peanut oil is ideal for deep-frying.

Take all the usual precautions where peanuts are concerned and avoid it if cooking for anyone with nut sensitivities. Use olive oil flavoured with a little sesame oil as an alternative.

Pepper, Black
Botanical name: *Piper nigrum*

Family name: *Piperaceae*

Pepper, the berry of a tropical vine native to India, is green when immature, and red or yellow when ripe. Black pepper is obtained by boiling and then sun-drying the green, unripe drupes. It is only used in some curries, but is an important ingredient in *garam masala*. Vietnam is the main producer of pepper.

Plum Sauce
A spicy, sweet Chinese sauce made from plums, chillies, vinegar, spices and sugar. Use as a dip. It keeps indefinitely in an airtight jar.

Preserved Melon Shreds
Also known as 'sweet pickled cucumber', these are thin shreds of melon preserved in a ginger flavoured syrup. They keep indefinitely in an airtight jar.

Red Colouring Powder
A brilliant red powder sold in Chinese grocery stores and used very sparingly to give the distinctive colour seen in barbecued pork. Substitute a bright red liquid food colouring if unavailable. Powdered annatto seeds or paprika may be substituted, although the red they produce is not nearly as vivid.

Rice Paper
Thin circular or square sheets of rice paste imprinted with a basket weave from the bamboo mats they are dried on. In their dry state they are very brittle and may shatter when dropped. After dipping in water they become pliable and may be used to wrap a variety of fillings then eaten as is or deep-fried. In Vietnam, these translucent wrappers are known as *bahn tran*. Unrelated to the fine, wafer-like 'rice paper' used in confectionery, which is actually not made from rice at all.

Rice Vermicelli
Sometimes labelled 'rice sticks', these are very fine rice flour noodles sold in Chinese grocery stores. Soaking in hot water for 10 minutes prepares them sufficiently for most recipes, but in some cases they may need boiling for 1–2 minutes. When deep-fried they swell up and turn white. For a crisp result, fry them straight from the packet without soaking. Also known as: *mei fun* (China); *beehoon, meehoon* (Malaysia); *mee sooer* (Cambodia); *sen mee* (Thailand); *bún, lúa min* (Vietnam).

Sesame Oil
The sesame oil used in Chinese cooking is extracted from toasted sesame seeds and gives a totally different flavour from the lighter-coloured sesame oil sold in health food stores. For the recipes in this book, buy sesame oil from Asian grocery stores. Use the oil in small quantities for flavouring, not as a cooking medium.

Sesame Paste
Sesame seeds, when ground, yield a thick paste similar to peanut butter. Stores specialising in Middle Eastern foods sell a sesame paste known as *tahini*, but this is made from raw sesame seeds, is white and slightly bitter, and cannot be substituted for the Chinese version, which is made from toasted sesame seeds, and is brown and nutty. A suitable substitute is peanut butter with sesame oil added for flavour. Sesame paste is sold in tins or jars; it keeps indefinitely after opening.

Sesame Seeds
Used mostly in Korean, Chinese and Japanese food, and in sweets in other Southeast Asian countries. Black sesame, another variety known as *hak chih mah* (China) or *kuro goma* (Japan), is mainly used in the Chinese dessert, toffee apples, and as a flavouring *(gomasio)* mixed with salt in Japanese food.

Shiitake Mushrooms, Dried
Botanical name: *Lentinus edodes*

Also known as 'fragrant mushrooms', the flavour of these mushrooms is quite individual. They are expensive but give an incomparable flavour. Soak for 20–30 minutes before using. The stems are usually discarded and only the caps used. There is no substitute. Also known as: *hed hom* (Thailand); *cindauwan* (Malaysia); *doong gwoo, leong goo* (China); *khô nm shiitake, nm ro'm khô* (Vietnam); *kabuteng shiitakena pinatuyo* (The Philippines).

Sichuan Pepper
Botanical name: *Xanthoxylum pipesitum*

Family name: *Rutaceae*

Often referred to as anise pepper or Chinese pepper, this is one of the ingredients of five-spice powder. Sichuan pepper is made from the dried berries of the prickly ash tree and is reddish-brown in colour. The shiny black seeds, which are very gritty, are discarded and the husks are used. It is easier to do than it sounds, as shaking the packet of peppers will make the empty husks rise to the top. They can be lightly roasted in a dry frying pan, pounded or crushed, then sifted and mixed with salt for a salt-and-pepper seasoning. It gives a tingling sensation when placed on the tongue. Also known as: *faah jiu, hua chiao* (China); *sansho* (Japan).

Sichuan Vegetable
Mustard cabbage (*gai choy*) preserved in brine, with chilli added. It can be used as a relish, or included in dishes requiring piquancy and tang. Sold in tins.

Soy Sauce
Indispensable in Asian cooking, this versatile sauce enhances the flavour of every basic ingredient in a dish. Different grades are available. Chinese cooking uses light soy and dark soy. The light soy is used with chicken or seafoods, or in soups where the delicate colour of the dish must be retained. Always use *shoyu* or Japanese soy sauce in Japanese cooking. In Indonesia, *kecap manis*, a thick, dark, sweetened soy, is often used. As a substitute, use dark Chinese soy with black or brown sugar added in the proportions given in recipes. All types of soy sauce keep indefinitely without refrigeration.

Spring Onions
Botanical name: *Allium cepa* and *fistulum*

Family name: *Liliceae*

Also known as scallions or green onions in some parts of the world, this member of the onion family is known as 'shallot' in Australia, but is correctly called a spring onion almost everywhere else, although the term 'scallion' is popular in the United States. Spring onions are the thinnings of either *Allium cepa* or *A. fistulum* plantings that do not form a bulb. They are white and slender, with green leaves, and are used widely in China and Japan. Also known as: *cōng* (China); *negi* (Japan); *phak boua sot* (Laos); *daun bawang* (Malaysia); *sibuyas na tagsibol* (The Philippines).

Spring Roll Pastry
Thin, white sheets of pliable pastry sold in plastic packets and kept frozen. Thaw and peel off one at a time (unused wrappers can be re-frozen). Large wrappers of the won ton type cannot be substituted.

Star Anise
Botanical name: *Illicium verum*

Family name: *Magnoliaceae*

The dried, star-shaped fruit of an evergreen tree native to China and Vietnam, it usually consists of eight segments or points. It is essential in Chinese cooking and is one of the key flavours in the stock for the Vietnamese rice noodle soup, *pho*.

Sweet Bean Paste
Made from soy beans and sugar, this paste is used in sweet steamed buns or Chinese moon cakes. Also known as *dow saah* (China).

Tangerine Peel, Dried
Sold in Chinese grocery stores, this gives an incomparable flavour to food. Substitute fresh tangerine or mandarin peel, or orange zest.

Tapioca Flour
Also known as tapioca starch, it is made from the dried washings of the cassava root. The flour provides a crisp coating on foods that are fried and is used in making many Asian sweets. Used to make sago and tapioca pearls.

Tofu
There is an abundance of varieties of this versatile soy product available. Fresh tofu, or bean curd, is found in the refrigerator section of Asian grocery stores and most large supermarkets. It comes in many forms: silken, soft or firm. Silken tofu is sweeter and more delicate than firm tofu, with a different texture and flavour. Once opened, tofu will keep for 2-3 days in the refrigerator if immersed in cold water that is changed daily. Dried bean curd is sold in flat sheets or rounded sticks and needs no refrigeration. It has to be soaked before use — the sticks need longer soaking and cooking. Deep-fried tofu puffs are also available. Red bean curd is much more pungent than fresh bean curd, and has a flavour like smelly cheese. It is sold in bottles and used in certain sauces. Also known as: *dow foo* (China); *tofu* (Japan).

Walnuts
Botanical name: *Juglans regia*

Walnuts used in Chinese dishes should be the peeled walnuts sold in Asian grocery stores, as the thin skin (which turns bitter with cooking) has been removed. Avoid black-skinned walnuts, and if peeled walnuts are not available, use either fresh California walnuts or the tinned, salted walnuts also sold at Asian grocery stores; the latter do not need further cooking.

Water Chestnuts
Botanical name: *Eliocharis dulcis*

Family name: *Cyperaceae*

Used mainly for their texture in Asian cooking. Sometimes available fresh, their brownish black skin must be peeled away with a sharp knife, leaving the crisp, slightly sweet white kernel. They are also available in tins, already peeled and in some instances sliced. After opening, store in water in the refrigerator for 7–10 days, changing the water daily. Yam bean (*jicama*) may be substituted if water chestnut is unavailable. Dried, powdered water chestnut starch is used as an alternative to cornflour for coating delicate meat such as chicken breast when deep-frying, as it helps lock in the juices. Also known as: *ye thit eir thee* (Burma); *pani phul* (India); *tike* (Indonesia); *haeo-song krathiem; haeo cheen* (Thailand); *go nung* (Vietnam); *apulid* (The Philippines); *mah tai* (China); *kuwai, kurogu-wai* (Japan).

Winter Bamboo Shoots
See bamboo shoots.

Won Ton Wrappers
Small squares of fresh noodle dough available at most supermarkets and Asian grocery stores. They can be refrigerated for up to 1 week if well wrapped in plastic, or can be wrapped in foil and frozen. Sold by weight, there are approximately 60 wrappers to a 300 g packet.

Wood Fungus
Botanical name: *Auricalaria polytricha*

Also known as 'cloud ear fungus' or 'jelly mushrooms', wood fungus is sold by weight, and in its dry state looks like greyish black pieces of torn paper. Soaked in hot water for 10 minutes, it swells to translucent brown shapes like curved clouds or a rather prettily shaped ear — hence the name 'cloud ear fungus'. With its flavourless resilience it is a perfect example of a texture ingredient, adding no taste of its own but taking on subtle flavours from the foods with which it is combined. Cook for only 1–2 minutes. Also known as: *wun yee* (China); *kikurage* (Japan); *kuping tikus* (Malaysia); *kuping jamu* (Indonesia); *hed hunu* (Thailand).

Yellow Beans, Salted
Very similar to tinned salted black beans, but lighter in colour. Use in dishes in the same way as salted black beans. *See black beans, salted.*